the geography of faith

the geography of faith

underground conversations on religious, political and social change

DANIEL BERRIGAN
ROBERT COLES

Walking Together, Finding the Way

SKYLIGHT PATHS PUBLISHING

WOODSTOCK, VERMONT

The Geography of Faith:
Underground Conversations on Religious, Political and Social Change
30th Anniversary Edition
© 2001 by Daniel Berrigan and Robert Coles
© 1971 by Daniel Berrigan, S.J., and Robert Coles
Originally published by Beacon Press

Library of Congress Cataloging-in-Publication Data
Coles, Robert.
The geography of faith : underground conversations on religious, political, and social change / Robert Coles and Daniel Berrigan.— Expanded anniversary ed. / with a new afterword by Daniel Berrigan.
      p.   cm.
Earlier ed. entered under: Berrigan, Daniel.
ISBN 1-893361-40-3 (pbk.)
1. Berrigan, Daniel. 2. Coles, Robert. I. Berrigan, Daniel. II. Title.
BX4705.B3845 A294 2001
261.8'0973'09047—dc21
2001034222

10 9 8 7 6 5 4 3 2 1

Manufactured in the United States of America

Walking Together, Finding the Way
Published by SkyLight Paths Publishing
A Division of LongHill Partners, Inc.
Sunset Farm Offices, Route 4, P.O. Box 237
Woodstock, VT 05091
Tel: (802) 457-4000   Fax: (802) 457-4004
www.skylightpaths.com

We dedicated this book in 1971
to the children of
North Vietnam and South Vietnam,
then enduring a terrible war;
and now we reach out to
children all over the world—
their lives, we earnestly hope,
full of expectation
and promise.

Contents

Daniel Berrigan in 1971
(photo courtesy of Bob Finch of Black Star)

Robert Coles in 1971
(photo courtesy of William V. Anderson)

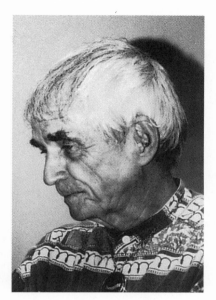

Daniel Berrigan today

Robert Coles today

Introduction to the 2001 edition

by Robert Coles

Each book has its particular life, and each awaits the new readers the passage of time provides. It is hoped that this new edition of *The Geography of Faith* will enable today's readers to travel back across three decades to experience that time when their nation was going through a significant conflict. By now, for many, the political and social travail of the Vietnam War is a matter of history—though some who fought in that war, or opposed it, or resisted it with all their personal might, are very much still with us, their memories a continuing collective record of that time when a powerful democracy had become a nation culturally and morally divided.

What follows should give readers approaching this book for the first time a fairly vivid sense of the climate of that time over a generation ago, when a devout Catholic priest, a Jesuit poet and teacher, decided to stand up to the American version of the "principalities and powers" mentioned in the Bible, and consequently was pursued by federal officials and their police agents—hence the word *underground* in this volume's subtitle. A person of relative privilege, a person devoted to religious activity and contemplation, became a hunted fugitive. It was a situation that not only changed one priest's life, but that symbolized a turnaround in his country's social attitudes: a topsy-turvy state of affairs it was, when a clergyman could become a fugitive from federal authorities, and it caused countless citizens to stop and think as they never had before about their relationship to their own country's policies, and even about their very allegiance to their nation's executive and legislative leaders.

How well I remember the conversations that came to make up this book, and how clearly I still remember hearing a particular commentary on them from my fellow psychoanalyst and wise mentor Erik H. Erikson, in whose course I was teaching as an assistant at the time. Professor Erikson followed the decision Father Berrigan had made with great and sympathetic interest. And it was to him I turned for support when my wife, Jane, and I decided to stand beside Father Berrigan, stay the course with him, and ask him to stay with us (an action itself in violation of the law, as in the phrase "harboring a fugitive from justice"). Professor Erikson was then studying Gandhi's philosophy of nonviolence as it had been lived out by him and his followers in British-controlled India.

One day, as we sat in Professor Erikson's Harvard study recording the conversations, the august and attentive and reflective Erikson asked that I stop the tape recorder so that he could pose some questions to us, and so, I later realized, that he could think carefully about what he'd been hearing. "I hope you will put all this on the record," he said (though at that point neither Dan Berrigan nor I knew what we intended to do with our conversations). I promised him that I would do so—make of the talks some kind of written record. We then listened to Professor Erikson's discourse on history, no less, and on those who witness it and become involved in its workings, the very stuff of his long-time research interests:

"You both are *saying* a lot for us to hear and consider, but I'd like to say here that what you are telling us, the words you send each other's way, are about *seeing:* each of you is, right now, an eyewitness to a history that is taking place before your eyes, the two of you, of course, but also before the eyes of your fellow American citizens—and maybe others who watch this country so closely for obvious reasons, its world-wide influence.

Some people will learn through reading what it meant to belong to a country and worry about its direction—to disagree with its direction. You and Father Berrigan may believe that it's your duty to dissent (in his case), and some would disagree with what you both have said or concluded—with your assumptions and assertions—while others would take a step further, and wish that Father Berrigan had been caught, right away. And so, there'd have been no such conversations as these which you're about to make available to the rest of us who read magazines and newspapers and books. A friend of Gandhi's told me this (I thought of what *he* said while I listened to what the two of you said): 'We were all trying to figure out what to think, what to do [with respect to the British laws and powers as they were enforced in India], and one day Gandhi spoke up, he said we had to act, and then our words would take on a new shape—they would follow our deeds and be given a life,' he said, 'by what had been done.'"

There followed a silence, as Professor Erikson seemed far away, his eyes looking beyond the room where we sat, and his head lowered, almost as if he were doing something more than just remembering those words. Finally, he returned to the subject at hand: "You are always mentioning fate, chance, drawing on your friend George Eliot [whose novels I like to teach, and consider eminently desirable and worthy companions, and so, yes, "friends," in a certain way] and I think now is the time for someone to mention that fate and chance and circumstance have offered Father Berrigan and you a time, a time to be together and to think about history itself, about what can happen to us as we live our lives, and events take place, and, well, catch us up in them. As I'm always saying, 'history and the individual'—but that is an abstract statement, and you two are offering a witness to history, I'd call it, some comments on life, as it gets engaged, sometimes with the world's changing events, and sometimes with its turmoil, its conflicts."

Then an even longer silence, as we both thought about what Gandhi had said in comparison with our own conversations,

Father Berrigan, a Jesuit priest on the move with his government in pursuit of him, pausing to make sense of his hopes and fears, his concerns and purposes, and I, an American citizen, his wife and children in a room only a few feet away, pausing in his own way to wonder what ought to be done by others like him—a nation's people then in considerable doubt, confusion, apprehension, with no small amount of felt misgivings becoming a daily matter of public discourse.

Finally, this from Professor Erikson: "You have had your say to each other, and now is the time, the 'historical moment' I keep mentioning, the occasion, to bring others into this conversation you've both had—so that today, and tomorrow, and in future years, when all this will be over, will be part of the past...then, years from now, this will be out there for people to try to understand—a part of our country's twentieth-century history to be studied, a lesson, you could say, to be learned, so that future events will, perhaps, be viewed with events in mind like this recent series of events we've all been through. We learn from one another, even as I think you and your priest friend have tried to learn about life's obligations and responsibilities—and possibilities, too—from one another; and I think you both may have been speaking with others in mind as well as yourselves, and others who will be born, as well as those now alive. That is what articles in magazines or in books do: the words of the writers become constantly available to readers—to stir or prod them, to give them a second's pause, or even longer sometimes."

Small wonder that I went back to these observations now, when this book is yet again being sent forth—a book that chronicles a trying episode in a trying time for a nation, when an overseas war cast its loud and compelling echo across a divided country, for a while seemingly at war with itself—so that individuals like Father Berrigan gradually, then forthrightly, became stirred to vigorously-expressed and -enacted political dissent (throwing their own lives willingly, eagerly, into a social confrontation with the powers that be).

Meanwhile, there were others who took these dissidents into their homes, took sides with them, or yearned to do so, or feared doing so, but yearned not to be under the control of such fears—those who were considering what ought to be done, and when, and why, in the course of one's life as a citizen of a democratic society. At stake for many were matters of belief, of faith, of conviction, of social and cultural and political adherence. After all, playing it safe can sometimes turn into playing it wrong, even as those who take on the established order can sometimes miss their mark and go seriously (and sadly) awry. And so it has gone in history, even as many of us keep wondering about our respective roles and responsibilities as citizens—all of that a subject of no small significance to Father Berrigan and his conversational friend back then in the seventh decade of this past century, a century understandably called, by many historians, *American,* by dint of our strength. Hence, the contemporary requirement that we as citizens think long and hard about the rights and wrongs about our country, and about our duties with respect to them.

Introduction
to the 1971 edition

by Robert Coles

In early July of 1970 I was visited by several young doctors, who wanted me to join with them in a public protest against the way the United States government was choosing to confine Father Philip Berrigan. A priest, an avowed pacifist, a man whose "crime" was to burn draft board records in protest against the way we have been fighting in Vietnam, Philip Berrigan was being held in Lewisburg maximum security prison in north central Pennsylvania. I was handed two pieces of paper, one a statement by Philip Berrigan himself, explaining why he had undertaken a fast and been sent to solitary confinement at Lewisburg; the other a pledge of support for Father Berrigan and young David Eberhardt and a call to protest by Catholic antiwar activists. The statement by Philip Berrigan was as follows:

STATEMENT
from Reverend Philip Berrigan, S.J., Lewisburg Federal Penitentiary

Since arrival at Lewisburg Federal Penitentiary, the prison administration has harassed me in the following ways:

1. Classified me arbitrarily as a maximum security prisoner for absconding on April 9—the rationale being that if we ran once, we would run again. Normally, every war pro-

tester goes to minimum security—Allenwood or Lewisburg Farm.

2. Placed me under suspicion of organizing a penal strike for
   no reason.
3. Shook down our quarters (allegedly to gain evidence for
   involvement in the strike); actually to seize personal
   writing—then employed to charge me with circulating
   contraband information in and out of prison.
4. Interfered constantly with mail, through overcensorship,
   through returning to sender otherwise legitimate mail,
   through attempting to trace my brother through my mail.
5. Encouraged informers (inmates) to report suspicious
   words, actions, and associations.
6. Issued a memorandum to the guards to watch me as a
   dangerous organizer.
7. Placed me on medium security as a phase to one of the
   farm camps. Then withdrew me to close security after
   shakedown of quarters and discovery of alleged suspicious
   material.
8. Refused to allow my niece to visit me, though she was
   getting married and departing to Germany for two years
   with her husband.
9. Searched me in the yard with no explanation. For what?
   A gun or knife, I suppose.
10. Searched the chapel sacristy (where I vest for Mass),
    possibly for firearms and explosives.
11. Putting me on report (with a certainty of punishment)
    for two minor violations, trivial enough to deserve no
    mention.

Taken singly, the above may appear inconsequential—together they form a climate of oppression under which no one can
humanly live.

The fact is, political prisoners at Lewisburg are persecuted
beyond the routine dehumanization given to the other inmates.
The rightist policies of the staff are proverbial, and they profoundly fear anyone standing for justice and peace. God, flag,

law, order, privilege—all mask a policy of falsehood to the men, petty persecution, and at worst, brutality of an impressive type. Meanwhile official propaganda boasts of rehabilitation—of tolerance, humaneness and creative innovation.

In reality, actual policy toward the men faithfully repeats the government's duplicity, broken promises and eager resort to naked force. The federal penal system is part of "big government"—one is no better than the other. Prisoners here are largely powerless, colonials not citizens, condemned for their crimes to the "crime of punishment"—from which there is little redress. They get the same essential treatment as blacks and Indochinese.

Personally, I didn't commit civil disobedience twice, submit to three mistrials and accept jail when I could have fled—all to abandon here my sense of justice and humanity. Nor to become suddenly, simply because I am under the power of "rehabilitation experts," a robot and a drone.

Consequently, I reject the punishment given me, refuse work and go to the "hole." There I will begin a fast for the men here, for Vietnamese and Americans in Indochina, for exploited people everywhere—and for their misguided, fearful and inhuman oppressors.

The further statement by Philip Berrigan's supporters read this way (Dr. Reuther is a Catholic theologian who teaches at Howard University in Washington).

Enclosed are two statements we have just received from Father Philip Berrigan and David Eberhardt who are serving prison sentences of 6 and 2 years respectively in Federal Penitentiary at Lewisburg for destruction of selective service files in Baltimore (4) and Catonsville (9). These statements have reached us through visitors to the prison. The men have been put into solitary confinement, and are fasting to protest their treatment in prison. We feel we should provide some background information in explanation of their letters.

Contrary to the general practice of keeping nonviolent prisoners of peace under minimum security, both have been kept under the regime of maximum security on the extrajudicial ground that the terms of their imprisonment will not be relaxed as long as Father Daniel Berrigan and Mary Moylan, also members of the same group, are not apprehended. That Father Philip Berrigan and Eberhardt are being punished for the continued resistance of Father Daniel Berrigan and Mary Moylan has been clear from the outset. Letters from these two prisoners and reports by visitors have indicated a pattern: whenever Daniel Berrigan has attracted public attention through his writings or interviews with the press and TV, and whenever the FBI has been particularly frustrated in its efforts to apprehend him, the ax has fallen on the two prisoners.

The ostensible reason for the prisoners' sentencing into solitary confinement on July 5, 1970, was their refusal to accept punishment for two minor offenses. These were: (1) standing without authorization for 5–10 minutes in the hallway following the Sunday, July 5, liturgy, and (2) reporting to what was purportedly the wrong lunch group, a mistake which was committed by ten other prisoners, none of whom received any punishment. But its actual background may be unknown to the victims. For example, the following events relate the treatment to which they are being subjected.

On June 27 approximately a hundred FBI agents, supported by a fleet of some 25 radioed cars and walkie-talkies invaded a wedding in a Lutheran church in Baltimore, Maryland, looking for Father Daniel Berrigan. The nave of the church, reception room, basements, and closets were searched. Guns jumped from agents' hips with the accidental popping of a celebrational balloon. The wedding was disrupted. Father Daniel Berrigan was not there. That the government agents' unprovoked invasion of the privacy and sanctity of a wedding produced no notice in the press, and little concern in the public, is a measure of our alertness to illegitimate executive behavior. Nevertheless, disruption of a wedding being a minor achievement for an expensive, well-mounted operation, the FBI agents had reason to be angry. The next day, Father Daniel Berrigan staring at the FBI from the pages of the Sunday *N. Y. Times* (Magazine) could not have assuaged their frustration. The captives in Lewisburg were bound to face the consequences.

We are writing to draw your attention to the unjust, extra-judicial character of the treatment of these prisoners. We urge you to publicize this information. By protesting these irregularities, we believe we are serving the public interest. The demands of the fasting prisoners are:

1. Transfer to the Lewisburg Farm or to Allenwood where they will serve their sentence under conditions similar to those of other prisoners of the Resistance.
2. Cessation of harassment of any political prisoners.

They request that we contact people outside requesting them to write letters and send telegrams to the Federal Bureau of Prisons, 101 Indiana Avenue N.W., Washington, D.C., to Warden J. J. Parker or Assistant Wardens R. L. Hendricks and W. H. Rauch, P.O. Box 1000, Lewisburg Penitentiary, Lewisburg, Pa. 17837. Also that we visit the Federal Bureau of Prisons and Congressmen and demonstrate at Lewisburg a week from today, July 16, 1970, at 2:00 P.M. If necessary further details on this demonstration will be circulated.

> For further information, please contact:
> Dr. Rosemary Reuther

I explained to the young doctors in my office, and to others (divinity students) who soon thereafter called me on repeated occasions from several cities, that I was reluctant to involve myself in an issue I really knew very little about. I was asked *why* I knew little about that particular issue. I was asked how it could be that I would even *consider* hesitating—in view of my past work with black and white youths in the South during the civil rights struggle of the early and middle sixties. I was asked to stop and think about what was *right*, not what was convenient to me. And anyway, what did I want to know that I couldn't be told, right then and there in my office by my visitors? Minutes became hours, and quiet discussion turned upon occasion into sharp, even bitter argument. I was told that my return North had ruined me, that I was becoming fearful and hesitant, that I was the worst possible thing, another "moderate," another "liberal" based in an "elitist" university.

In turn I tried to explain why I was unwilling to become involved in the effort those young physicians, among others, wanted to make. I outlined the work I was doing. I was (and am) working with black families in Boston's Roxbury section and with so-called lower middle class white families, by which I mean families headed by men who are policemen, firemen, factory workers, gas station owners, bank tellers, office clerks, schoolteachers. I started that work after years of living in the South (Mississippi, Louisiana, and Georgia) where I tried to find out how black children and their families managed to survive the mobs which harassed them when they pioneered school desegregation in that region, and how white children and their families responded to such challenges—and not the least, how young activists confronted segregationist customs, only to be themselves confronted by certain "last-ditch" defenders of the status quo, be they called Klansmen or sheriffs or members of citizens' councils. I have at some length described the kind of work I do (*Children of Crisis: A Study of Courage and Fear*); but in my office on that July day I had to emphasize what I believe must also be emphasized here: the range of people I see from week to week, and the consequent limits to my social and political involvements.

When I lived in Mississippi and started going from town to town, home to home, I worked closely with members of SNCC and CORE, but I did so as a doctor, a psychiatrist, someone certain youths wanted to talk with, and I did so only at certain times—because at other times I was talking with angry and hurt segregationists, frightened and outraged Klansmen. I have never had any doubts about where my sympathies and commitments are, nor do I believe the Klansmen I have talked with have had any doubts, either. Still, in 1961 or 1962 not all civil rights activists (and especially not all white youths who came South from states like California or Massachusetts or New York) could agree with these words spoken by a black Southerner to me shortly after he was released from a jail in Alabama: "Don't keep apologizing and apologizing for talking with the segregationists. We need bodies to put on the line in this fight, but we also need someone who can 'read' those white folks to us—the ones who scream and scream and hate and hate."

I had indeed been apologizing and he, in a much longer statement than I have just presented, told me to stop feeling that he would want to condemn me for this or that—stop, in a way, judging *him* by turning him into an accuser of sorts. Yet he knew then, as did I, how possible it is for those caught up in a hard social struggle to become self-righteous and moralistic and narrowly, punitively ideological. And in 1962, when those words were spoken, the scattered protests of sit-in students and freedom riders were being increasingly called a "movement"—a development which very much influenced the way individual activists got along with one another. A "movement" in its early stages is no rigid bureaucracy; nor is it an institution in the process of consolidating itself. A "movement" (or at least the civil rights "movement" I watched develop) is a somewhat loose and vaguely defined coalition of people, interests, and involvements —which at the same time can be seen to have an utterly precise purpose. Put differently, hundreds and hundreds of people labored at a variety of tasks in the South during the early sixties; and all the tasks were directed toward one goal, the breakdown of a region's entrenched segregationist social and political system. Nevertheless, the individuals in that "movement" held to a wide range of beliefs—and eventually that range would become apparent. Limited successes, after all, satisfy some, frustrate others, enrage still others. Defeats are accepted by one group as inevitable, felt as a serious disappointment by another group, and looked upon by a third group as the most outrageous and provocative thing imaginable.

Meanwhile, as "movements" broaden and begin to face the stresses within themselves (in contrast to the stresses the enemy exerts) one begins to hear "credentials" become a major issue. Who "really" belongs to the movement? Who is an outsider, an interloper, an opportunist, maybe even an informer? Who is using whom for what purpose? Especially when initial successes occur do such trends develop. To draw again upon some later remarks (1964) of the young black just quoted: "We're nowhere near where we want to be, but we're getting there—so we're no longer as united as we were. The way to kill a 'movement' is to give it enough rope to hang itself. I'm beginning to believe that. Up to last year we were all brothers together; now there are arguments and more arguments. Everyone has his own idea of what the 'movement' is, and people say bad words to each other, and there isn't the love we had for each other, and I wonder if that's what happens any time a lot of people get together: they make some progress, then they fall to name-calling and fighting."

We didn't exactly fight with one another in my office that July morning in 1970, but we did discuss at some length "the movement"—the civil rights movement and the peace movement; and again, some sharp words of disagreement were spoken back and forth. I was reminded that I had visited activist youths in Southern jails and publicly protested the way those who demanded the vote for blacks were themselves punished. I was reminded that I had written a number of articles about prisons and the injustices to be found in them. I said in reply that I was spending day after day with policemen and factory workers who do not easily give their trust to one of my ilk—and who would (I feared) react strongly to any mention in the newspapers of my involvement with those who condemn the government and its foreign policy. I said that I simply can't have it both ways; that is, I can't join a group of upper middle class liberal-to-radical intellectuals and expect even so to be welcomed unreservedly by already suspicious and troubled men and women, who feel ignorant and insulted every day by the "left-wing college crowd," to use one expression I so often hear.

Eventually we agreed I would bring up the whole issue with the families I work with, and see what they thought, what they felt someone like me should do. So, the next day I asked a thirty-seven-year-old policeman what he knew about the Berrigan brothers. Nothing, he replied. I told him what I knew. Then he did experience "a bell ringing somewhere." We talked and talked, and I believe a shortened version of his reactions deserves to be set down: "I think the college crowd, the left-wing college crowd, is trying to destroy this country, step by step. They're always looking for trouble. They're never happy, except when everyone pays attention to them—and let me tell you, the ordinary people of this country, the average workingman, he's sick and tired of those students, so full of themselves, and their teachers who all think they're the most important people in the human race. Now a priest is a man of God. My brother is a priest. I have two aunts who are nuns. God calls men to be priests. I can't believe you can be a priest and a Communist. The two don't go together. I think some priests make mistakes, but I wouldn't want to be the judge who sends them to jail. Of course, in this country if you have a lot of money, the chances are you won't go to jail, or if you do, you won't be there for very long. The poor are the ones who go to jail—and I know, because I've been a policeman for fifteen years, and I've watched what goes on in those courtrooms. I pity anyone who hasn't the money to buy himself an experienced lawyer.

"The colored are no good, most of them. A lot of them are in jail, and let me tell you, they belong there. I don't trust any of them. The rich liberal crowd, they've gone nigger-crazy. But, they don't see what I see. They talk about those 'poor, poor colored people'—and sometimes I just wish they could meet the 'poor, poor colored people' I see in the lineup. They go crazy. They go after each other, *each other*, not only the white man, with razor blades and knives. They are the meanest people alive.

"I'll say this, they're dumb; so you can't blame them alone for all the trouble they're having. They're being egged on by all those college professors and their schemes, and by the students.

Sometimes I wonder how the country is still in one piece. And even the Catholic Church is getting caught in all of this. When I was a boy the Church stayed out of all this political trouble. Now you have these priests running around and sounding off on everything, every damn thing.

"Of course, I'll say this: there's a lot of injustice in this country. The rich don't suffer much, whether we have inflation or a recession. It's always the little guy. And meanwhile, the college kids go to Africa or over to the nearest colored section, and say they're worried over this and worried over the next thing—but they don't worry about millions of their own people and all the troubles we have. They're all for the North Vietnam government, but not their own. They'll prefer anyone's side to America's side. It's the lousiest business, and I have to watch myself when I'm on duty and they start their demonstrating. They're looking for trouble. They have the dirtiest mouths I've ever heard. I thought I was bad! They're teaching me new words all the time.

"I ask you: how could a priest ever get caught up with such people? I really wonder if he hasn't been brainwashed, this Father Berrigan. How else can you explain it, when two brothers start getting involved with people like that, the whole 'peace crowd,' and all their noise and troublemaking. To them the flag is a rag. To them a cop is a pig, and they have a new swearword for us every day. To them this country is the enemy, and so is the Church. That's why I say this: if a priest gets caught up with them, I can only feel sorry for him. If I were you I'd go and try and talk with the priest and tell him he's got himself all mixed up, and he should stop and look around and see what's happening. And in this world it happens all the time: the clever ones, who are no damn good, take advantage of the nice, innocent guy—whose heart may be in the right place, but his head isn't, that's the trouble."

From others who live not far away from that policeman I heard somewhat similar remarks. On the one hand I heard the government and its policies stoutly defended; on the other hand much dissatisfaction over a whole range of injustices was expressed. For several days I hesitated. I look back now and try to understand why, and I am still not sure why—but I think my mind at the time was so completely taken up with the feelings and wishes and fears of the families I was (and still am) visiting that I felt unable to become involved publicly in something they would take issue with strongly. For five years I have been working with those mothers and fathers and children, and I know how betrayed they feel—at times, they say, by just about everyone and everything in the nation. It seemed important then and continues to be important that I be as candid as possible about my views and involvements and purposes—all of which I was told one evening in July by a man who works in a gas station and holds strong political opinions: "You have to be honest in this world. My dad taught me that, and I've tried to follow his example. I feel sorry for a lot of the people I talk with at work. They're businessmen. They're professional men. And I'll tell you what else they are: they're liars. That's right, they are so scared they keep their thoughts to themselves and say only what they think the other guy believes. I get to know these characters over the years, and they come clean after a while. One man told me he doesn't really have any political beliefs. He said he sizes up the man he's talking with, then blends in his own ideas to that man's ideas. Can you beat that? I may be poor compared to guys like him, but at least I speak my mind, at least I'm *that* free. Of course, with some people it's best to shut up and not get into arguments with them. What's the point? You just drive customers away, and pretty soon you're out of a job.

"I can't help feeling this would be a better country if we all leveled with each other. I don't hold a man's views against him, so long as he tells me what they are. The trouble with this country is that the politicians who run it learn to talk out of both sides of their mouths. I don't believe 90 percent of what they say; that's right, 90 percent. All you have to do is look at them and listen to them long enough and you can see that they're a bunch of clever, tricky characters who will do or say anything to get elected and stay in office. That Lyndon Johnson, did anyone in this country really like him? I'd hate to think of how many lies he's told in his life. The same goes for Nixon. They're all alike, slippery as they come. Like I tell you, George Wallace at least speaks right from his heart, and tells you what he believes. I would have voted for him if I didn't think I was wasting a vote. The Democrats are more for the working man than the Republicans, I know that; so I stick with the Democrats. But I don't think they're that much better.

"Politicians call themselves statesmen, and they tell you that because they've got themselves elected to some big-deal office, you're supposed to look up to them and admire them and not say anything bad about them. Meanwhile they wheel and deal and cover up on this and say one thing here and another there and go back on their own words, if they have to, so as to get elected. I guess it's our fault for paying any attention to them in the first place. But what are you going to do? You have to vote for *someone*. That's why I say: if that Catholic priest is an honest man, he shouldn't be locked up in jail. He's probably a damn fool; but I'll bet he's more honest than some of our big-time leaders—I'll bet he's not out to line his own pockets and become a bigger and bigger fish in the ocean. He's probably an idealist, that's what. And let me tell you: the world doesn't like idealists.

"If I was you I'd go and talk with the guy, and tell him he should go back to being a *priest,* and stop this political agitation business. He's way above his head. He can't win against our politicians and the big boys behind them, the fat cats. So, why should he try? And the Communists are always standing by, waiting to pick up the pieces. They're a bunch of murderers. The trouble with a priest who gets into politics is this: he'll never get any place changing this country; and he'll be playing into the hands of the Russians—and as bad as our politicians are, at least they're not dictators. You ought to go visit that priest in prison, and let him know that. Tell him politics and religion don't mix. Tell him the Russians love to see signs of trouble in this country. And tell him he's wasting his time, because this country is run by the big industrialists, and the politicians who do what they're told to do, and the big-mouthed professors (they're all so swellheaded) who are always whispering advice to people—as if they know how the world works! That's what I say: tell the poor father to mind his own business and get out of prison and speak honestly to his flock, but stay away from politics and things like that—or else he'll start sounding like a crook himself. All politicians learn to sugarcoat the truth; they just don't talk straight from the shoulder. I guess they look down on the ordinary American workingman. I guess they don't trust us. I guess they figure they can con us, all the time con us."

After I had finished speaking with him I decided I would try to go ahead and visit Philip Berrigan in prison. I began to call colleagues of mine, among them Dr. Karl Menninger and Dr. Seymour Halleck, both of whom have for years been consultants to the Federal Bureau of Prisons, and Dr. Willard Gaylin, whose book *In the Service of Their Country: War Resisters in Prison* gives a sensitive and compelling account of how conscientious objectors manage in prison. Dr. Gaylin in particular was no stranger to the Lewisburg Penitentiary. For many months he had visited men there or in the prison farm nearby. He warned me that I was in for a Kafka-like experience—if indeed I was allowed a visit at all. After a number of phone calls, including one to Norman Carlson, the Director of the Federal Bureau of Prisons, I was granted permission to visit both Father Berrigan and David Eberhardt. Philip Nobile has described some of the bizarre kind of rudeness I encountered there in the course of a prolonged discussion with the warden ("Senator Goodell and Philip Berrigan," *The New York Review of Books,* November 5, 1970). Yet, for all the difficulties I encountered at Lewisburg I was able to get some sense of what was happening to the two men I spoke with for part of a morning and most of an afternoon. Upon my return home I wrote up a psychiatric report on each man and sent copies of the reports to a variety of people: the attorney general, Mr. Carlson, Senators Goodell and Kennedy, and a number of my colleagues. Upon my return home I also had to deal with a letter from the chief of the Prison Bureau's psychiatric services, written the day I was at Lewisburg and before I had had a chance to finish talking with Philip Berrigan and David Eberhardt, let alone settle in my mind what I saw and believe to be true. I believe the reader ought to see the exchange of letters between Dr. Barr and me.

UNITED STATES DEPARTMENT OF JUSTICE
BUREAU OF PRISONS
Washington 20537
Division of Health Services

July 20, 1970

Robert Coles, M.D.
Coolidge Road
Concord, Massachusetts 01742

Dear Dr. Coles:

Dr. Halleck called me this past Friday (July 17), and I am aware that you are at Lewisburg penitentiary today. With such flimsy credentials, I am sending you literature describing the activities and/or programs during the past year of nine Bureau psychiatrists, plus a paper of my own.

My reason for providing you this material is to try to provide a perspective which I think you will otherwise be unaware of. It is easy to criticize government institutions; prisons are easiest of all. Such criticism often requires little knowledge and no courage, and is destructive in its result. But to be constructive requires some degree of both courage and knowledge.

Forgive my pompousness, but I respect your professionalism as exemplified for instance in your paper on Morgantown. It is distressing, however, when some people, otherwise knowledgeable, say and write things which are self-righteous, self-aggrandizing, and destructive to their manifest goal.

I trust I have described my position clearly. With best wishes, I remain

Sincerely yours,
Norman I. Barr, M.D.
Enclosures   Chief, Psychiatric Services

HARVARD UNIVERSITY
UNIVERSITY HEALTH SERVICES

75 Mt. Auburn Street
Cambridge 38, Massachusetts
August 3, 1970

Norman I. Barr, M.D.
Chief, Psychiatric Services
Division of Health Services
U. S. Department of Justice
Bureau of Prisons
Washington, D.C. 20537

Dear Dr. Barr:

I am replying to your letter of July 20. I thought it was a rather unfortunate letter for you to send to me. As you yourself indicate, I have tried in the past, in many ways, and in many articles I have written, to be thoroughly fair to the Federal Bureau of Prisons, and indeed have singled out various projects that the Bureau of Prisons has undertaken for particular praise. I have already spoken to you for two hours, from nine-thirty to eleven-thirty on Thursday, July 23. I hope that as a result of our conversation you will not continue to think about my visit to Lewisburg in the way you seemed tempted to think about it in your letter to me. As I explained to you, over twenty-five young internists, surgeons, and psychiatrists came to see me over a period of several days; they all were concerned about what was happening to Father Philip Berrigan and David Eberhardt, and they asked my help. They asked my help because they knew that I had been involved in a number of social issues in this country over the past ten years, and to be blunt, they were asking me to do this, or perhaps stop writing articles about prisons or indeed about many other issues. If they are self-righteous, as you are afraid I might be, then I can only thank God for that kind of self-righteousness; because as you yourself acknowledge, there is indeed a need to look into some of these difficulties, and in fact to be thoroughly critical, in the best sense of that word.

With respect to the words "courage" and "knowledge" that you summoned, I can only say that I have no real interest in calling myself either courageous or knowledgeable—or being called so by you or anyone else. What matters to me in this case, and in many other cases, is whether men are suffering when they should not be suffering, or hurting when they ought not be hurting. The facts are really what we need, and if those facts become bothersome to you, or indeed to me, then perhaps we will look at ourselves as closely and with as much scrutiny as other nonviolent dissenters have in the past. I have in mind men like Mahatma Gandhi, Dr. Martin Luther King, and Cesar Chavez. Men like that have also been in prison, and no doubt been both critical, yet full of courage and knowledge.

I don't know whom you have in mind when you talk about "some people, otherwise knowledgeable," who are saying and writing "things which are self-righteous, self-aggrandizing, and destructive to their manifest goal." I wish that you could have been more specific and clear in that particular portion of your letter. Who are those people? How have they been self-righteous? How have they been self-aggrandizing? What destruction have they wrought upon what goals?

I must confess that I am deeply troubled that you should have written the kind of letter you did to me on the very day that I was at Lewisburg, before I had a chance to talk with you, before you had any indication about why I was there or what I might be hoping to accomplish when I arrived there. And since you yourself mention that you had read an article of mine which was thoroughly approving of a major project that the Bureau of Prisons has undertaken in Morgantown, West Virginia, I am even more puzzled by the tone of your letter.

In any event, I am taking the liberty of sending to you two psychiatric reports I have written up; one deals with my im-

pressions about Father Berrigan, the other about David Eberhardt. As you know, we discussed much of this at great length
on the telephone. It was my decided impression that essentially
we were in agreement; I mean, that you were also concerned
about the grave threat to Mr. Eberhardt's psychological condition, and with respect to Father Berrigan, you appreciated the
depressive trend in his personality. As I recall, you thanked me
for using the word "depression" in evaluating what was happening to Father Berrigan. I also recall that in our conversation you felt that Mr. Eberhardt should be transferred immediately out of Lewisburg Penitentiary, and to either the Allenwood
Farm or the Lewisburg Farm. And you agreed with me that a
prolonged stay by Father Berrigan in a maximum security
prison would be thoroughly detrimental to the man's personality and state of mind.

Now, a week later, the men are still at Lewisburg; and I do
wonder what you think physicians like Dr. Willard Gaylin and
I ought to do that would be considered by you "constructive."

Sincerely yours,
Robert Coles, M.D.
Research Psychiatrist

The government by no means hurried to move David Eberhardt or Philip Berrigan out of the Lewisburg maximum security
situation. In late July and early August I spent most of my time
trying to impress upon various government officials my concern
for the two men, especially young Eberhardt. And in order to
reach the general public Dr. Gaylin and I wrote a letter to the
New York Times in which we tried to set down what we felt was
happening to the two men. Meanwhile I had again been con-
tacted by some young doctors, this time because they wanted me
to meet with Daniel Berrigan, who had then been underground
for several months. For one thing Daniel Berrigan had read
about his brother's fast, and was worried about him. But beyond

that, the forty-nine-year-old Jesuit poet and teacher wanted to talk with me for reasons best declared by him in the following statement, which was sent to me by him through intermediaries.

What follows is an attempt to set down, in no particular order, a series of topics for discussion. The subject matter, in the most general sense, revolves about "the movement" (discipline and practice) and psychology (idem). In view of the mutual distrust and distance that prevails, it might be of profit to open a dialogue. Distrust: from the point of view of the movement, young people are almost universally convinced that psychologists and psychiatrists devote themselves predominantly to those with the money to afford fees like twenty-five and thirty and more dollars an hour. Moreover, a psychiatric "cure" often can be this: the person "treated" eventually "adjusts" to the world around him. "Adjustment" is made to that which should in fact awaken rage, resistance, indignation.

It seems significant to radicals that while there are "movement" doctors, lawyers, priests, even (!) dentists, there are none or practically none of the forementioned gentlemen operating in the front lines of social change. The practice and style of psychiatry in particular does not seem to lend itself to the formation of a caucus of innovative leaders, in touch with the touchy Left, taking some equivalent risk, reporting back to the rest of us how it goes where the going is tough. Such psychiatrists would get in trouble (inevitably) with the Royalists.

What is health anyway? Who is to distinguish the sane from the insane? One thing is certain; no clue will come from the city morgue, and few clues from the suburban couch. Some clue might be offered from exposure to the edgy people who are trying for social sanity in the midst of madness-as-power.

What is the relationship between "health" and the nature of one's "community"; and between one's "community" and the action this world requires from us? What ought one's attitudes to be toward the law in lawless times? Can the man of conscience be considered a vindicator of legal tradition—in contrast with the hacks, fast-buck boys, militarists and racists who raise hob, here and now, with the irreplaceable and blood-stained legacy of human decency?

Then, there are other issues to think about. I set them down in abbreviated manner. Symbolic action vs. words, words, words. Life as inner truth. Panthers, resisters as human models in a time of drought. Celibacy, chastity as response and responsibility. Validity of insights of Gandhi. Relationship of "life force" to concentration on the task at hand. Unacceptability in American culture of a "minority within the minority." The religious person: his resources, world view, humanism, "grace under pressure." Life, death, rebirth. Inwardness, sacraments, prayer. Biblical man. Formulations of faith vs. the "confessing Church" in time of crisis. Universality of "body of Christ," "kingdom of God," "world body" images.

Time and consciousness. Resources and staying power of relationships. What do social ferment and chaos do to the continuum of consciousness? Of what value (harm) are the "peak moments" of dread, fear, violence and withdrawal (or ecstasy, hope and love) in making more of self available to self?

Can we call the movement a "school of alternatives." To many the "American experience" is a constantly narrowing cone of descending possibility, with death at its vortex. It would seem, to understate the case, that this need not be. But what can be? Tragic acceptance? Modesty? Need the sense of inevitable cataclysm be dismissed as sensationalism, apocalypticism, or is this simply a sober reading of the times, hence accurate? How do men get along who face death as near at hand, yet try to maintain a certain joy? What do they have to offer? The movement as a school of imagination—as relief from killing seriousness. One criterion: does the movement produce art, shelter artists, deviants, "useless" people, bums?

Nonviolence, politics; "efficiency" vs. the quasi-mystical long haul of history. Exemplary action as a social resource. "Suffering fidelity" of Bonhoeffer. Prison experience of practically everyone. Power (rejected) vs. powerlessness (chosen, inherited). Underground as symbol and reality. What happens to one's "head" living virtuously outside the law? What might this mean for others? How might the suppression of certain freedoms and functions lead to creation and release of others? Hopefully submitted.

I met with Daniel Berrigan and after a while we decided to record our conversations; no stranger to a tape recorder, I arranged to do so. Our meetings lasted several hours at a time, and extended over about a week. In between meetings we each tried to get straight in our minds what we wanted to talk about —though when we actually met and began speaking to one another we did so freely and without resort to notes or any agenda. After the taped discussions were typed up we each were going to edit our respective comments—but in mid-August Daniel Berrigan was arrested on Block Island, and so it has been left to me to do that work for both of us (Daniel Berrigan, as a federal prisoner, is prevented from working on any manuscript materials). I have tried to remain faithful to the spirit if not the absolute letter of our conversations. That is to say, I have for the most part kept intact the sequence of our respective remarks and changed words or phrases, or upon occasion sentences, only when an idea or a thought was otherwise not understandable. I have only rearranged those segments of our comments to each other that seem to belong together. The result is seven titled sections which (I hope) have a certain coherence. As I look back at what we said to each other I see that each of us kept circling around certain issues of concern to himself. When I started talking with Father Berrigan I viewed myself as a more-or-less "passive" listener, ready with questions and summarizing remarks and clarifications and words meant to stimulate an already talkative and sometimes eloquent priest. Yet, the reader will see that from time to time Father Berrigan would not let me keep on prodding him or tersely taking issue with one or another statement of his. Though it is not part of the record,

I was hesitant to talk at length about my own concerns and worries, and on several occasions said so just before putting on the tape recorder. But as we talked I became more and more "involved," as it is put these days. Daniel Berrigan is a strong-minded but not particularly self-centered person. He wants to talk *with* people rather than *at* them. He wants to persuade all right, even exhort; but he keeps a sharp eye upon his listener, and seems to desire (almost invite) a measure of disagreement. I found little of the ideologue in him, little of the wordy theorist. He could be unashamedly vague and uncertain and of two minds—which can be frustrating if one is bent on finding clear-cut "truths," but impressive if one distrusts all conceptual "systems" of thought, however self-assured and tempting.

About the time the agents of the Federal Bureau of Investigation were putting handcuffs on Daniel Berrigan the tapes had been fully transcribed; but for several months I had to leave the manuscript unattended, because I was finishing other work I had long ago started. I tried to write to Father Berrigan at the Danbury prison, but my letters were promptly returned. He was thoroughly locked up. In December of 1970 I began the work that has enabled this book to appear. I also requested from the warden of Danbury a chance to see his Jesuit prisoner, and was finally granted that chance. In January of 1971 Father Berrigan seemed less gaunt than he had been a half-year or so earlier and very much at ease with himself. His sense of humor was undiminished. There was, still, an open, warm, somehow childlike quality to him. When I asked him what he was "doing" in the prison, he told me that he was working as a dentist's assistant: "I am discovering a whole new world, the world of the mouth." When I asked him to look at the edited manuscript I had carried with me, he agreed to do so and did so, but right off was characteristically trusting and generous: "I am glad you have done the work, and I am sure you have done a fine job." I told him I wasn't so sure. I told him I had tried to remain loyal to his manner of speaking, his poet's mind—but that upon occasion I had to expand upon his taut, compact sentences and at the same time thin out some of his metaphorical expressiveness. I was afraid that in so doing we now *both* sounded cautiously evenhanded, nervously restrained. "Well, at times I *was* that," he said, "and at other times maybe I was given to moments of overconfidence, or for that matter, the opposite: a kind of pessimism about the world." In any event, he felt we had during those days at the end of July 1970 worked *toward* something, and done it together—"felt one another's presence" were his words; and so he had "no reservations at all" about sending the manuscript to the publisher.

I have not felt so unequivocal—and perhaps that difference of attitude reflects larger distinctions between the two of us. As I have read over the text of our remarks to each other I have worried that somehow we emerge as vulnerable, indeed, easy prey for those categorical minds who would want to have one speaker the "liberal" or "moderate" who hems and haws, and one speaker the "radical" who questions everything and has little sense of the price that any society must ask of its various members. And I have worried, too, that as I go over the pages of the record of sorts to follow, and write this introduction, I will be tempted to dominate the conversations themselves with a long and overwrought and slyly self-justifying apology. After all, Father Berrigan is in jail; I am free. Father Berrigan dares take on the richest, most powerful government in the world (admittedly *his* government, *our* government); I worry at what is happening in Washington and shake my head over what has happened in Vietnam and know in my bones after all these years what goes on every day in the Mississippi Delta or up the hollows of eastern Kentucky or in a Boston ghetto—but beyond that do nothing. Oh, I write; I try to capture sights and sounds, set them down for others (hopefully) to meet and get to understand. Still, I don't march, don't take to the streets in indignation and horror at what my country does or doesn't do. If anything I tend to fall in line, more than fall in line. Unlike Father Berrigan, who has lived in Europe and Latin America and traveled through Asia, I have never left the United States. Perhaps because I have stayed so resolutely at home on this continent, I am ignorant of what might be, what *is* in other nations. Perhaps I am a victim of the patriotic rhetoric so many of our loudmouthed politicians use to dull our sensibilities and distract us from their treachery and deceit and self-aggrandizement. Perhaps I am a coward, pure if not so simple; that is, perhaps all the complexity and ambiguity I can't stop calling to mind enable me to hedge my bets ever so carefully in the face of any serious and threatening risks.

I say all that not because I believe it, but because I have for many years heard such charges made by people toward other people. In this regard, I do not speak of myself, though I have always known that accusations made by one group of people against another have a way of spreading and spreading, especially in moments of crisis and alarm—and God knows, the late sixties have not been easy years for this country. At no point did Daniel Berrigan make me feel (let alone suggest that) his life and mine in some way had to be *compared* with one another, *set against* one another, viewed as a means of judgment or condemnation. There was about the man a real willingness to accept differences and emphasize common involvements, concerns, struggles. Yet, again, I know full well how the kinds of observations both he and I have made in this transcript of a particular series of talks can be taken up and "interpreted" in God knows what way for God knows what purpose. Since I believe a million words of explanation and amplification will not prevent such a development from coming to pass, there is no need for me to make this introduction very long. I do, however, want to say this: it is important to me that Daniel Berrigan and I could talk as we did, day after day, without rancor or distrust; rather, we enjoyed going at again and again certain issues that obviously plague us. We repeated ourselves. We left a subject and then came back to it in a different way. We agreed. We did not at all agree. We stated things, then qualified or retracted what we said. And all the while, I believe it fair to say, we enjoyed the experience a great deal.

And at the end I suggested to Father Berrigan that the policeman and gas station owner I quoted from early in this introduction might find it interesting to talk with him. They knew he was underground, yet both men (and their wives) had told me they would be happy to spend an evening with "the Father," as they called him. Unfortunately "the Father" had to leave, go elsewhere, preach in a church, bring himself nearer and nearer to the moment of capture he never considered as anything but inevitable, even in time desirable. Indeed, once as I was changing the tape, Father Berrigan said this: "I *have* to be caught, you see. If I never got caught that would mean I was hiding too much. The whole point of all these weeks underground is to stand witness all over—here and there, and God willing, everywhere possible. Caesar and Mammon are everywhere. So, it is everywhere they have to be confronted."

Another time, as I prepared to put a new tape into the machine, for some reason I felt a need to say some things. I emphasized what I had been saying "for the record" or "on the tape" about the meanness self-styled "movement people" demonstrate toward others nearby, let alone those who occupy different ideological or philosophical terrain. I said I was (I still am) sick and tired of hearing policemen called "pigs" and just about anyone called a "fascist." I was sick and tired of seeing the American flag insulted and abused. I was sick and tired of seeing the deliberate antics and provocations of various individuals tolerated and encouraged by many others—people who may denounce "conformity" in our "middle Americans" but have their own shibboleths, their own sacred rituals, and not the least, their own fears, so far as speaking out is concerned. If high public officials frighten many of us into acquiescence, then "radicals" too can be silenced and intimidated by the banalities and cruelties and obscenities of their various "spokesmen," if

not leaders. I never said all that when the tape recorder was going, at least not the way I have just written out my feelings. But
Dan Berrigan was not one to forget easily; so one of the last
things he said to me when we said good-bye in early August
was this: "I wish somehow our conversations could be expanded. I wish some of the families you work with could have
been with us. I wish their viewpoint could have come across
more continually as we spoke. They are in you, as you talk—but
someday I'd like to get to spend a good, long time with such
people. But who knows when that day will come?"

If questions like that last one seem a little fateful and dramatic, one can only say that the challenge Daniel Berrigan is
making to our society is just that—a forceful, surprising and
(for many) shocking one Nor has the latest (midwinter of
1970–1971) news done anything to diminish the nature of that
challenge. I have no way of knowing now (February of 1971)
whether the government has the slightest bit of evidence to
substantiate the charges it has made against the Berrigan brothers, among others. What is one to say months before a trial,
especially when nothing substantive has been released to the
public? Am I to come forth with a strong condemnation of the
policies and tactics men like John Mitchell and J. Edgar Hoover
have bequeathed us? That is not difficult to do. Am I to insult
Daniel Berrigan by at this point—before the reader has a chance
to read our remarks to one another—praising him extravagantly
and suggesting that martyrdom will soon be his? I fear that,
also, is not a difficult thing to do these days. But I have no wish
to demean a tough, knowing, complicated, lively, passionate
man with all sorts of unqualified applause—appropriately
timed to defend his "reputation" against the assaults of the
Department of Justice of the United States Government. (As
this book went to press in early May of 1971, the Department of
Justice dropped its charges against Father Daniel Berrigan. He
was no longer alleged to be a "co-conspirator" in the case.) Nor
do I have any intention of lining up in support of the statement
read by Mr. William Kunstler outside of Danbury prison—in

which he compared the government's latest action against the Berrigan brothers with the burning of the Reichstag in the early days of the Nazi era. In my opinion such allegations are unfair, thoroughly unfair, and they give an all too easy and gratuitous victory to the likes of those who now run our Department of Justice.

Though America in the sixties is not to be compared with Germany in the thirties, Christians everywhere and in every decade of every century have had to struggle with institutions. Christ urged guile on His followers as they struggled with the world. He acknowledged Caesar, at the same time insisting that His ways were not the world's ways—yet inevitably, it seems, He had to confront personally the power of those who ran an empire, not to mention those who ran a religion. No wonder, then, Daniel Berrigan mentions Dietrich Bonhoeffer from time to time. He and I never had a chance to discuss Bonhoeffer's theology, though he had in late May (already underground) written a long poem as a review of Eberhardt Bethge's biography *Dietrich Bonhoeffer,* and I had that spring been reading Bonhoeffer's *Ethics.* Like Simone Weil, Bonhoeffer is a hard person to call upon in a time of need—that is, if one wants "advice" or "help" in making a decision. Intense, conflicted in the best sense, full of doubts, yet stubborn and energetic and purposeful, he struggled hard to find God's grace. In her touching biography (*The Life and Death of Dietrich Bonhoeffer*) Mary Bosanquet offers this example of Bonhoeffer's thinking—taken from an unpublished lecture of his:

The Christian religion as a religion is not of God. It is on the contrary another example of a mortal road to God like the Buddhist or any other, although of course different in form. Christ is not the bringer of a new religion, but the bringer of God, therefore as an impossible road from man to God the Christian religion stands with other religions; the Christian can do himself no good with his Christianity, for it remains human, all too human, but he lives by the grace of God, which comes to man, and comes to every man, who opens his heart to it and learns to understand it in the Cross of Christ; so the gift of Christ is not the Christian religion, but the mercy and love of God which culminate in the cross.

One can see how leading Churchmen would find such talk impossible and threatening indeed. And especially one can understand the right of Catholic theologians to take issue with such a viewpoint. But perhaps Daniel Berrigan falls back on a tradition within his own Church that nourishes the kind of stubborn and admittedly treacherous individualism he admired in Bonhoeffer. During the days we spent talking he was working (late into the night) on an essay. He didn't want to talk about the writing he was doing, but he did take note of the presence among my books of Roy Campbell's fine translation, *Poems by St. John of the Cross*. St. John was of course a poet and a reformer. He was sent to jail at the behest of various "authorities" in his Church; his passionate efforts to help St. Theresa of Avila breathe life and spirit into the Spanish Church were too much for any number of proud and self-righteous Carmelite officials, who hounded him, persecuted him, called him a threat and a danger, locked him up—and drove him to further "resistance." More than anything else, St. John had the courage to trust his own, spontaneous, deeply felt love for God; trust that love enough to acknowledge it in one poem after another; trust that love enough, really, to take on the Church's powerful men, and even to lift his voice (and head and heart) toward God alone, God who is not a church or a religion but (as Bonhoeffer dares suggest) Himself, which means beyond all man-centered (hence inherently corrupt and corruptible) organizations, institutions, and ideologies.

It is, of course, easy for us in this century (and all too easy for one like me) to point out that a man like Daniel Berrigan would naturally "identify" with St. John or Bonhoeffer. And yet, a man of the cloth fleeing the civil authorities and aware that sooner or later jail awaits him, naturally turns to those others who have stood up and risked their comfortable, day-to-day "security" or "freedom" in the name of something higher and more important, in the name of Him. Still, as I saw him and experienced his mind and spirit, Father Berrigan had none of the self-conscious "leader" in him. He was not hoping that somehow Bonhoeffer would supply him with hints; nor did he hope that his experiences would in some way prepare his mind's already established lyrical side with new energy and momentum. He was looking for examples all right, but he spoke of his own life, like all lives, as unique—and he was not about to surrender *that* vision to a social scientist who would gratify something called his "charisma" or his "urge to greatness" by tracing for him the connections between him and other theologians or poets or political activists.

It is quite possible that some men on this earth carve out their own destiny, and only then, as they are well along, seek out across time and space the testimony of others. The issue is a man's desire for companionship, not his need to "identify" with someone, or imitate someone else. At stake is sequence, chronology—and quite possibly, one's view of man's nature. I believe Dan Berrigan came to Bonhoeffer and St. John of the Cross well prepared, very much himself, and *responsive* is the word—responsive out of his own rich and by no means settled life. It may seem an impossible jump from the early morning of December 14, 1591, at Ubeda, Spain, to the early morning of April 9, 1945, at Nazi Germany's Flossenbürg concentration camp, but a man alive in 1970 could do it quite unselfconsciously. I believe it no accident that our conversations ended, mysteriously it seemed, with St. Paul's "I die daily." The tape ran out then, even as time was running out; there were others to see, other things to do. But the man who spoke such words at the end of these "Conversations" had already in a way been with St. John in Ubeda when he died, been with Bonhoeffer in that Flossenbürg camp. Indeed, only later, when I went to Danbury prison, did I begin to understand how intimately Daniel Berrigan has lived with the "death" St. Paul mentions. Lively, warm-spirited, ironic, at once detached and very much *there,* he seemed so very composed in the visitors' room, hard by a guard—and so I couldn't help recalling what I had thought to myself a half a year before: he is afraid, he fears prison, he is on the run for *that* reason as well as other (more political, more philosophical) reasons. I do not apologize for having once had that kind of thought; it is not a surprising one, given my life and profession. As a matter of fact, even if Dan Berrigan had been afraid, the substance of his "stand" against the United States Government would have to be argued out on its own merits. But in Danbury I realized I had been wrong; as a psychiatrist, one interested in figuring out what goes on in the minds of those I "see" and "talk with," I had failed during that midsummer week to comprehend the man—and most likely, attributed to him my own inclinations, my own hesitations and worries. Daniel Berrigan was not enjoying prison. He was not "happy" there, and he was not "depressed" there; he *was* there—naturally almost, as a matter of course almost. Nor did he act like a martyr. And anyway, I suspect it is us, the onlookers, who set aside the Bonhoeffers or Berrigans of this world by conjuring up "martyrdom" for them. That way they are special; it is not their deeds which challenge us, but their "psychology" which intrigues or fascinates us. And no doubt about it: intrigue or fascination are easier to bear than self-scrutiny.

When I came back from Danbury I finished work on the last section of our "conversations" and prepared to write this introduction. As I was doing so the news of the government's conspiracy indictment broke, and as I have already indicated, I have found myself unable to say much about all of that—except that I cannot reconcile the coming pages of this book with what I have read in the papers or heard on the radio. So, I have instead turned my mind to less immediate matters. I have read Bethge's biography of Bonhoeffer and Mary Bosanquet's briefer but powerful version of the same man's life. I picked up again

Bonhoeffer's *Letters and Papers from Prison* and went through, once more, the poems of St. John of the Cross. For some reason I kept going back to this of St. John's: "I cast off my costly garments,/ Donned the working clothes you see,/ And the harp that was my music/ Hung upon a willow tree." And among Bonhoeffer's words I kept going back to this:

But if someone sets out to fight his battles in the world in his own absolute freedom, if he values the necessary deed more highly than the spotlessness of his own conscience and reputation, if he is prepared to sacrifice a fruitless principle to a fruitful compromise, or for that matter the fruitless wisdom of the *via media* to a fruitful radicalism, then let him beware lest precisely his supposed freedom may ultimately prove his undoing. He will easily consent to the bad, knowing full well that it is bad, in order to ward off what is worse, and in doing this he will no longer be able to see that precisely the worse which he is trying to avoid may still be the better. This is one of the underlying themes of tragedy.

Who can struggle to make this world more decent and avoid such dangers, the makings of such a tragedy? As I have looked over what Father Berrigan and I were moved to say to each other I have sensed (only in retrospect) that a good deal of our time and energy was taken up with a discussion, direct or implicit, of the warning Bonhoeffer sets forth so compactly and unnervingly. Over and over again I worried about Daniel Berrigan's assumptions, his way of seeing things, his acts; and over and over again he reminds me that because I seem, compared to him, inactive does not mean I am not taking a stand, perhaps alongside those I claim to condemn—and that stand is predicated on a whole range of attitudes and beliefs, some of which I may not care to spell out very closely for myself. Bonhoeffer would never want to interrupt a life at any given point and take it upon himself (or suggest it is the responsibility of any other human being) to decide whose life is decisively headed for the kind of tragedy he speaks of; but Bonhoeffer wants to warn us, warn himself, that we all ought to stop every once in a while and look things over—look at just what we are doing, just where we are going. And for helping me to do that in the summer of 1970, I can only be grateful to Father Daniel Berrigan.

Finally, I hope this particular "conversation" will draw the reader to Father Berrigan's writings, his books of poetry, like *Time Without Number* and his more philosophical and theological essays like *They Call Us Dead Men.* And for those readers so inclined, a growing "literature" has responded, as it were, to this one Jesuit's words and deeds. I have in mind the entire issue of *Christianity and Crisis*, Volume XXX, Number 15 (September 21, 1970); and *Holy Cross Quarterly*, Volume 4, Number 1; and one issue after another of *Commonweal*—for example, its August 7, September 4, and October 2 issues; and of course, Francine du Plessix Gray's *Divine Disobedience*. As I have read what others have said about the man and his various ideas, I have realized how consistently he moves any number of us to anger, outrage, confusion, admiration, affection. A man of culture and refinement, he has lashed out at the academic and artistic world. A man versed in logic, and in many ways an obvious rationalist, indeed a skeptic, he can become all of a sudden mystical. I never wanted to "analyze" his personality, but its complexities kept appearing and never quite resolved themselves; I suspect they will grow and grow and become the full-blown paradoxes that significant lives so often present to us.

Meanwhile the rest of us (who live further away from the "edge" Daniel Berrigan keeps mentioning) will hopefully now and then demand of ourselves at least a measure of what he seems unable to spare himself—and I refer not to suffering or sacrifice, but the hard work of loyalty to the God Isaiah and Jeremiah called upon, the God in whose name Jesus Christ walked and spoke and taught and healed. It is, again, not for one living man to decide what another living man's worth will be when it is all over, when all of us alive are gone and the light of that Judgment Day the Bible speaks of begins to fall upon us.

But for better or worse the Reverend Daniel Berrigan, S.J., has never lost his loyalty to his fellowman and his God. He may have erred; he may yet err. He may have said unwise things; he may yet do so. Nearing fifty, a prisoner, very much alive, "in the middle way," headed for more notoriety and conflict (right now that is surely clear), he will not want to stop being among us, he will not want to let go of us—until one day he is told to do just that, to leave here and to go there, to become part of God's scheme of things in a way no living man can really imagine, let alone talk about. I fear it will only be then (as is so often the case) that many of us will dare acknowledge what we have all along had in such remarkable abundance in one man.

Cambridge, Massachusetts,
February 1971

1 • Families

Daniel Berrigan: I suppose I might say that today was a typical day in the underground—and after a number of weeks one feels able to make a remark like that. I was up last night with some friends until about two in the morning. We were talking about what the last months have meant to us. Today it was especially striking to be handed my brother's book, which has just been published, and having an opportunity to go over some of the anguish and some of the experiences of the past months that have in a sense separated us very much. He is in prison now. But at the same time I feel a real sense of solidarity and unity with him, knowing that we are both called in different directions. I have also heard reports from Baltimore that the FBI showed up in force and with drawn guns at a wedding of two movement people. They searched the church. They raided the rectory nearby. And I have tried to understand such violence on their part—which I'm sure is compounded by their personal frustration at what I am doing—yet knowing, on the other hand, that I have no guns, the people I am with have no weapons; I don't believe I have ever held a gun. I wouldn't know what to do with a gun if I had one.

Every day now I wonder what we are about, what we are trying for. I think it is hard for those who are in power to understand what it is we want—they come after us with guns, and we want only to demonstrate how violent so much of the world now is. Recently I have felt the way I believe many of the Panthers have felt so continually, and the way our young war resisters have felt, and the way others in the movement have felt—that the violence is from the other side and that often those who say they are for "law and order" turn out to be mean and greedy, and determined to hold on to their power with guns.

I was reading today those very touching pages written from prison by my brother Phil—the first priest in America, as far as we know, to become a political prisoner. I was struck by his very calm effort in the midst of a difficult time to be analytic, to show his understanding of how things are in America, and to create something, to create something truly for the future and for all of us. My brother wants to live "on the edge," so to speak; he wants to live with all kinds of ironies and even absurdities. And perhaps I should go over some of the ironies and absurdities, some of the reasoning, some of the sensibility that led to all of this.

Robert Coles: To all of what?

Berrigan: To being in the underground at present, where it is quite clear that something is happening to me and something is (I believe) happening to the others with whom I am staying and spending my time; and maybe the "something" has to do with the development of consciousness—that could be one way of putting it. It seems fairly certain, as far as one can be certain in very obscure times, that like it or not my brother and I are involved in a struggle for a certain kind of moral awareness; and it also seems that the moral questions we are trying to raise cannot be raised in the traditional way—at a polite "debate" or in a "discussion" at a "forum." I am in jeopardy, and it is from such a position that I hope to discuss and use moral issues. Back in the spring when the prospect of prison became a certainty, I felt very strongly (and so did my friends) that some of us ought not sit back passively and let the powers-that-be have their victories, one after the other. We felt that we had to persist in raising moral issues we felt involved in, and place our lives in jeopardy.

Our ideas developed in stages. First we thought we would perhaps just make one gesture. There was, I remember, a weekend of political exchange and of music and poetry at Cornell, when I met with the nonviolent movement. About two weeks before that meeting I went to a meeting of some friends, including some of the Catonsville Nine; there we tried to discuss the prospect of going to jail—make ourselves aware that it was soon to happen. Eventually I agreed to do this: I would join a temporary underground around Cornell and then appear at the festival, which would be a kind of enlargement of the idea, the idea of nonviolent resistance to things our nation is doing here and abroad. In those days of solitude in which I was with a family in a farmhouse in northern New York State it came to me in the course of prayer and reading that this was not the end, that I was not going to surrender, but rather try to see what I could do as a person willing to take risks with his own fate in order to talk with others and help himself and those others think about the terrible problems we have, and the new approaches to living we must find. So I proposed that I go on—I did so to my friends, who were surprised, because they had looked upon the weekend as the turn-off point of all this. They thought I would turn myself in or get picked up, and maybe part of me did, too.

Coles: It was your idea to stay free, or as free as someone being hunted by the police can be?

Berrigan: Right. When I appeared there that night before those people in that crowded arena my friends came to me again as I was on stage; they said they had the means for me to leave at some point if I felt inclined to, and I said yes, that I should go, rather than turn myself in to the police. I feel stronger than ever that the whole thing is extremely important, that I have learned a lot and shared a lot with people who have wanted to open themselves up to new ideas and feelings. I am more determined than ever to continue with this kind of life, for all its hazards, as long as it is possible. I believe that this experience is valuable not only for me but for those with whom I stay, those who offer me hospitality and accept me in the best way, by talking with me about the serious problems our world now faces.

Coles: I gather you have been talking with a wide range of people, with many families.

Berrigan: Right: with people who have been in jail as conscientious objectors, with people who are weighing their future course of action as political activists, with communications people, with artists and poets and teachers. Perhaps there is a historical need for it, for a man like me to confront himself and others he gets to know—as well as to confront society.

Coles: Are you saying that the underground which you have had access to, in the course of the past three months, has enabled you to meet with many people in many cities—and still you are not caught?

Berrigan: Yes. I never wanted *only* to be a fugitive—to stay out of jail *only* for the sake of staying out. That was never, never the idea. I wanted to stay out in order to take risks. If not, then I might as well go to jail and remain there.

Coles: What do you think has happened to the people you've been staying with—I mean, apart from the "personal" thing that has developed between you and them?

Berrigan: Well, it has been the feeling among many families, and especially the families of professional people, that some crisis of conscience or breakthrough takes place as we talk. For instance, I feel that we've done some hard thinking about the family as a fundamental social unit. As I talk with wives I hear them express their sense of isolation; they feel condemned by the present social system, and they feel isolated from one another. They have many concerns as women and human beings —and there is no one listening to them, not the way people listen to politicians and others who always sound off. We must explore ways of sharing talents, of sharing in the rearing of children, the care of the home, the earning of money. I had felt the need for such changes before I went underground, but now I feel stronger about the issue—perhaps because I've been at home so much, with one mother after another! Many of these families are beginning to embark upon what we in the Church call newly developing "retreats." In these retreats there is the chance, especially on weekends, to get together with people either in the underground or fresh from jail, and explore together some of these matters, so that the family need not indefinitely be a frozen unit—at the service of the war-making state, the service of the consumer society—and so that all the energies and vitalities which each of the members represents can be released again.

I think that today young people come toward marriage as growing, searching men and women; and suddenly marriage and parenthood is represented as a stoppage of all that. I mean, young married people become members of a social community, and come under the authority of a political community. Once children come, even some of our more radical youth feel themselves no longer so free to protest various wrongs—because they need work and on their children's account feel more dependent on, more vulnerable to, the power of a town or city or county. They are expected to join with other consumers. They are expected to prepare the next generation for the next wars and for an expansion of the same, the very same community.

Coles: Are you trying to say that the family as we know it in the West is in a sense an agent of the political system that you oppose?

Berrigan: Yes, I am saying that.

Coles: How do you as a Catholic priest deal with this issue? How do you deal with your Church's feeling about the integrity and almost inviolacy of the traditional, so-called nuclear family? How do you reconcile the Church's thinking with your psychological ideas of what is valuable for people—and I presume children, too, although we'll have to get into that later, I'm sure.

Berrigan: Right. I think the Church as I have experienced it during, let's say, thirty years of membership in my order, the Church is speaking less and less to the realities before us. Just one instance is the Church's failure to face and deal with the social and political difficulties of believers. And then when one moves out to another scene, as I have been doing, and meets the people of very mixed religious and ethnic backgrounds, one sees how tragically unresponsive the Church has been—because it has not heard and been moved by the ethical struggles of people on the "outside," yet maybe nearer to Christ's own struggle. More and more I see the need for flexibility in the Church. And I feel that one's responsibility to the Church can no longer be expressed by the priest's or parishioner's traditional compliance before powerful and sometimes corrupt "authority." I would like to see the resources of the Church brought to bear upon the realities that the Church alone cannot deal with—though it can shed certain light upon many troublesome issues. It is such matters I am discussing now with the families I stay with. I hope we can come upon something new, which will help us in the very real and new situations we are facing. I hope there is a spiritual breakthrough of sorts awaiting us, so that we can learn to live together in a new and stronger and less "adjusted" way—"adjusted" to the forces in America which plunder other countries and our own country as well.

Coles: Could you spell out a little more what you are talking about with the families which are offering you shelter?

Berrigan: What we are proposing is that at some stage these families actually begin to get together in important ways—and feel the strength and protection of one another's presence and commitment. The danger I want at all costs to avoid is that people now working as one will simply revert after I'm gone to the kind of private islands on which they were living before. They themselves have remarked that sheltering me has been important to *them*—a means of helping them grow and face and make certain choices. I hope they will move further toward those choices on their own.

Coles: Are you in a sense an evangelist going from home to home, hoping to help these people in certain directions—as human beings, as well as politically?

Berrigan: Well, Dr. Martin Luther King was often accused of coming into a certain situation and introducing or causing violence. In reply he would say that he was merely unmasking what was there all the time—the violence, the hate, the exploitation. He merely allowed to come to the surface things that were on everybody's mind anyway. That is to say, there were hatreds and racist attitudes of a very ingrained kind and suddenly, because he was there and because he was interested in trying to speak the truth forcefully, all sorts of people were talking more than ever—and it *was* very disruptive and violent, and there *were* dangers of all kinds; but it was also good, very good, and it lasted. There is an analogy here without pushing the analogy too far. I mean, a stranger who comes into a household is sometimes able to mention and bring up certain issues otherwise ignored or glossed over—so long as there is a mutual agreement with the family that he is really wanted there, and wanted as a person with ideas, be they right or wrong. So, I think I've been able to help some of the families I've stayed with to think about their position in our society, their human responsibilities—and I think they have given me a lot to think about, too.

Coles: What you are saying is that your radical situation now —your relationship to American society and your relationship to the government, to the courts—is a situation that demands for its maintenance a radical community; and that you have in the weeks of your life underground met with others who have been willing to talk with you, exchange ideas with you, to an extent share your fate by taking certain risks—and in general *be* with you.

Berrigan: Right.

Coles: In that sense they take a step with you. Your presence among those people compels a kind of self-scrutiny that might not be possible for them were you not there, were your position among them not a given.

Berrigan: I can see where this movement is a kind of uneven advancing wave—almost like the progress of a person on a surfboard, the movement is going to have different features at different times, but it seems to me that the subterranean or mid-ocean forces are so profound and powerful and unknowable even that one can never conceive of himself as though his own wave were an inch or a foot. Words can only be suggestive here, but I see us working for a new "ecology"—of man and his way of living with other men. We are being carried toward destruction or toward a new creation; and so the wave hits the shore in different ways, with different impact from place to place. We are facing something that only occurs, it seems to me, rarely within the stretches of time, and so I do not believe I should be isolated as a single phenomenon. I just don't belong to myself. I belong to my own convictions and in the very working out of my own convictions I continually find companions—because my experience is common to today's man. It may be at one point or another that I reason this or that "publicly," you could say, but others have been doing likewise, and we have all been waiting for each other. Look, to be very practical, from the very beginning of our movement it was not that we were going to say no to this or that phenomenon, the brutality of this or that outrage, but we were trying to propose styles and alternatives in a time of war and turmoil, alternatives that were not merely saying *no* to what was outraging us—rightfully we felt. Our no was a yes, which means that our saying no to death was our saying yes to life. Our effort had to be embodied, had to be embodied personally by our bodies and minds. We were seeking after hope, "visible points of hope" I once put it to myself. I suppose we became those points for some people, some families, my brother and I did.

Coles: Must the family be the stumbling block you feel it to be?

Berrigan: I see the American family as an institution in the same impasse that the churches are. These are obviously very clumsy reflections, but if we are talking about which structure in our society seems to offer the greatest resistance to change I would say, yes, it is the family. I don't mean that the family isn't changing; I mean that in a consumer society, the family is the means by which most people become tied to a cycle like this: go along with things, so long as you get enough to buy more and more things even though the whole world is exploited so that a relatively small number of people in this country—*us!*—can live well. (Our own land and air and water are also plundered in the interests of the same kind of blind consumerism.)

Coles: What you would say, therefore, is that what keeps someone like me from being more sharply critical of our society is not so much the various ideological rigidities of my profession, or the way it lends itself subserviently to a certain kind of social system, and in fact allows itself to be used as a means of judging people within that system—by calling them mad if they are social critics and calling them deviants if they express their political resistance too strongly, in short by calling them all kinds of psychological names which are really politicized names and pejorative names. Again, you are saying that it is not such things that really count. You claim it is because I am a husband and a father that I am cautious. In another sense of the word I "husband" my resources and remain loyal to the system, the social system, the economic system, out of fear, out of trembling for my children. I become increasingly tentative and cautious as I try to bring my children up, get *them* into the system, preserve for them the privileges I've inherited or won for myself. Furthermore (if I follow your line of reasoning), as a burgher of sorts I've learned to control carefully my mind and its particular persuasions, its beliefs. Regardless of how sincerely I hold my opinions, in the clutch I hold them not out of sincere and open-minded conviction but because I *have* to—as a landowner, a householder, a husband and a parent who lives a comfortable life in this particular nation. Hence I am very cautious indeed about criticizing this society too broadly, too vigorously, too thoroughly. After all, I want all its advantages—for my children, of course! So, I carefully, maybe semiconsciously, calibrate how far "out" I dare go politically. Is that what you're saying?

Berrigan: Yes. And I think marriage as we understand it and family life as we understand it in this culture both tend to define people in a far more suffocating and totalizing way than we want to acknowledge. There is very nearly universal supposition that after one marries one ought to cool off with regard to political activism and compassion—as compared to one's student days, one's "young" days.

Coles: Married men to a degree lose their social compassion?

Berrigan: Yes. Many of them feel that after marriage their interest in social issues has to be "extracurricular." Admittedly I am not married, but still I see no reason why, in the nature of things, what I have just described *should* be so. I see why things are as they are now, in this particular country. But I think things are changing. I have to get vague here, even a little mystical, some might say—but it seems to me that the biology of the spirit is really exploding in this country, hence the inner turmoil that is all around us today. Biologically and spiritually we are trying to break through to another stage of human development. I think we're in a period when on the one hand everything in the culture seduces us into nonexperimentation or into irresponsible experimentation which is the same thing, and on the other hand something deep inside us says we've got to live differently, not in one little fiefdom after another on one plot of land after another. We have signs about us: the communal experiments of students and of younger people, for instance. More and more one hears that the goods of the world belong to the world and that the parceling out of these things into arbitrary units is not even helping us, let alone other people. More and more one hears people question what the *point* of all this acquisitiveness is. The sharing of life, the sharing of goods, the sharing of spiritual experiences is becoming something important to our young. Drawing on the experience (for example) of David Miller, who was married before he went to jail—they had one child and the second on the way—I see no reason why the political and religious passion of a man like him should be dampened by the fact that he is now a husband and a father. Indeed, because his wife shared his views, because he and his wife were protected by a larger community, his going to jail I believe marked a period of real growth in the man. I'm obviously not arguing here that it was *good* for David to go to jail; but worse things have happened to people outside of jail—because there was not a community around them and because they were simply caught up in the cruelties and exploitations of our society.

Coles: So you are not really arguing against the family *per se.* What you are arguing for, what you are saying, is that a husband and wife can maintain their own sense of privacy with their children and yet also maintain a kind of political passion which you think necessary.

Berrigan: I would think so. Again, I hope I am not arguing abstractly or as a priest who doesn't know a thing about the demands of marriage. I'm arguing as one who knew well the married members of the Catonsville Nine; they were with me and I with them, and I saw what married people could do, together, and in defiance of what all those commercials on television show going on between husbands and wives and children. Maybe man at the peak of manhood is most revolutionary, and his passion for change may live side-by-side with marriage, or he may want to postpone marriage. I don't think he *has* to stay single, though.

Coles: You're saying that *some* men at the peak are revolutionary. Clearly, many aren't.

Berrigan: All right, let's say I'm talking about an ideal man, a heroic kind of man.

Coles: Talking about *some* versus *many*, I'd like to ask what one thinks or does about a nation whose people, perhaps like people everywhere, are mostly not "ideal" nor "heroic"—in this case a nation whose majority is comfortably enough situated to be reasonably content politically. I guess what I am saying is that I think we are basically a very conservative country. I think that by and large the people in this country are conservative, do not want radical change of any kind, are well fed, well housed, and on the whole satisfied with things as they are. Not that they don't want changes here and there; but in the main they feel satisfied with the life they have, and unwilling to have you or me or any other smart-aleck intellectual come along

with our brainy ideas, so often spoken so damn self-righteously
and with such damn condescension. I have to contrast the way
someone like Herbert Marcuse writes about the ordinary working class man in an industrial society like America and the way
those men and their wives and children actually talk about
themselves and their life. To read some social critics, life is so
dreary and empty and routinized and fearful in our lower middle class suburbs. To read them, drones live there. I wonder
how many factory workers Marcuse spent time with before he
constructed those elaborate theories of his. I wonder how much
time he took to witness lives, the everyday lives of people. I
see joy and humor and affection and liveliness among the working people I visit in their homes; they are not the people some
of our radical critics would have them be.

In any event, your remarks remind me of a book called *Centuries of Childhood* by Phillipe Ariès. He tells us that the close-
knit, bourgeois family is a recent phenomenon—one that appeared in the last two or three hundred years and in response
to the development of Western industrial civilization. I was
thinking of his book as you talked about the uses to which
American society has either consciously or blindly (probably
both) put the family. In certain respects, as you say, the American family now is a consumer unit the likes of which the world
has never seen; and the family certainly can become—here or
maybe anywhere—a rallying ground for traditional forces. After all, as one becomes a family man one often does, as you
said earlier, put aside political interests and instead make a series of adjustments, accommodations, compromises, arrangements, the sum of which sap one's spirit. The result is less interest
in social protest, less effort to stay politically aware, less anger
and outrage at the world's injustices. It is interesting that many
young protesters have taken to new arrangements with one another, whether it be the communes or a kind of *camaraderie*
that really brings and keeps people together. I saw such issues
develop in the early sixties in the civil rights movement. It became clear that in order to continue that kind of social protest,

the status of the private lives of the protesters at some point would have to be confronted as much as the segregationists would have to be confronted. And it's interesting in Israel now: in a society which has practically had to insist that all of its people live urgent political lives, live at the edge of survival even, the kibbutzim have emphasized new ways of childrearing, new ways of communal living.

Berrigan: I think it's very important to consider the relationship between the American family and American life in general. One of the things that many American children are denied is exposure to human variety—and then there is the fact that many of our children are taught to hate, not only taught so in homes, but by sheriffs, mayors, governors, and on up. Then, our children, so many of them, are taught to close the doors of their homes, barricade themselves from others and instead fill their own coffers with one purchase after another. I may be over-simplifying, but it does seem to me that, as the saying goes, we are what we eat, and that's a cultural statement as well, which means the kinds of families that have been "flourishing" in this society for a hundred and fifty years, especially in the white middle classes, have become what they have embraced: consumerism; militant self-interest; and wars to subdue "natives," obtain international power, and control various governments. I take it as crucial that the child from the beginning have before him or her a wide variety of possibilities. The child should know well many kinds of people, not only the two people who have produced him or her; and exposure to what we might call many "models of manhood" should continue right through, be present in the schools and playing fields and colleges.

Coles: Models of Motherhood and womanhood, too.

Berrigan: Yes. Take the university; it seems to me that in many of our universities the impoverishment of the human spirit continues and really becomes acute. I mean, the young are isolated in those places, and kept among their own age-mates, and also kept from the real problems of the world—not only in other nations, but right across the railroad tracks from the university buildings. Whatever the rhetoric, it is quite clear that many professors have no interest in their students, or want no dealings with them beyond the coldest, most impersonal kind of academic arrangements. In many universities the teachers cling to power and the young feel vulnerable, and words like "human fraternity" are spoken by tired and hypocritical old presidents at graduation exercises in the hopes that the alumni will feel good. No wonder some of our young are so enraged. I have often noted that the metaphors which have governed dealings with the young are military metaphors—which may be why so many dormitories have had the awful, colorless, cheerless look of army barracks. And families, too, can be virtual armies: the child is segregated, indoctrinated, isolated in order to be injected with a world view. Armies, and all too many homes and schools, discourage real freedom of expression, freedom to think broadly, roam widely through books and ideas. And armies succeed, as do many of our homes and schools: lives are controlled, spirits crushed, wars of one kind or another waged and won. But children pay for those victories. We all do. We become indifferent and self-centered—the very enemy of Christ's spirit of sacrifice and love for all mankind. No wonder we get frightened when our children rebel. We are afraid they will catch on, rise up in rage at the deceptions and tricks we have played on them, in the interest of "adjustment." I can conceive of a different kind of world, in which a youth's rebelliousness would be considered desirable and as natural as childbirth itself: it is up to growing children to surpass the moral understanding and the world-awareness of their parents, and further rid us of the vestiges of violence and racism and the rest; it is the child's fate to move ahead of us, rather than be the one upon whom we dump all the filth and detritus of history, in the sense that our children are supposed to grow up and fight wars, and continue to live "apart from," say, blacks or other groups.

Coles: Regardless of whether one agrees or disagrees with what you've said, I wonder how the cycle you speak of can ever be broken in millions of instances. I assume you wouldn't advocate any forceful rearrangement of family living, and I assume you are hoping that examples can be set here and there by groups of people—examples which in some way will be infectious or contagious or inspiring, so that other families will join in the kinds of arrangements you advocate. But as you were just talking I kept thinking of the families I now work with—they are white workingmen and their wives and children, people now called "middle Americans." They are fiercely loyal to a certain ethic, elements of which they don't often spell out for themselves, let alone any self-conscious "observer" like me. They are indeed parochial—and would not consider the word an insult if it were used to describe them as "to themselves," so to speak, and desirous of being self-sufficient. They can be competitive, standoffish, truculent with respect to next-door neighbors, let alone foreign countries, and proud of their turf, even if it be a quarter of an acre, bordered by other quarter-acre lots. Now I don't mean to be perversely pragmatic, but I just wonder: how are we going to reach and "change" such people? Perhaps that isn't a question you or anyone ought to be asked. But I do wonder whether it isn't possible for intellectuals to become so theoretical, so haughty, so self-righteous, that they lose all contact with the realities of life, which in this case means the kinds of lives and values millions and millions of people cherish, and will not give up without one hell of a fight. Most children in any country, let's face it, are not going to have the moral and ethical alternatives that you're talking about handily given to them, either by the school system or in the home. And by the time those children become teenagers they are indeed ready to march off to war. We all are (or most of us are) ready to march off to war. We feel loyal to the government. We call ourselves citizens of the country. We are mobilized quickly by the President, by the maneuvers of a particular administration—and off we are, waving the flag and ready to do and die.

Berrigan: Well, *some* of us are. I think that your analysis really has to be subject to the facts of this war. Obviously there are many many thousands who form a nucleus of hope for a different future, and have come through this war with a profound kind of rebirth of the spirit. You know, I don't at all hesitate to be a bit utopian about all this because I think hope is itself an act, a very big leap, which in a sense defies the grim facts always about us and opens up new ways of thinking about things. So, this war has caused thousands to leap, and in so doing see the possibilities of a different kind of world. I think it's going to be harder and harder for many of us to continue the same old confidence game with ourselves. We have been moved to look at dozens of things that as well-to-do, comfortably "moderate" or "liberal" people we never wanted to see, and could always brush under the many rugs our money and education enabled us to own. Now we are in a more precarious position, a more significant position, some would say a fatuous one—but I believe we are strong and alive as we never before were.

Coles: I'd like to go back and ask you how you hope (as a person somewhat hunted and exiled within your own nation and living within what could be called an underground) to reach out to particular families in such a way that they will be moved to look carefully at themselves and what they as a family are doing and what they as a family believe?

Berrigan: I didn't have that hope in the beginning; I didn't know what was ahead. But gradually I have begun to have such a hope. Living with families as I must during this period of being underground, I have tried to enter each home as a quiet member of a growing discussion—one my presence naturally triggers, because it is a moral decision for a family to accept me, a man sought by the FBI. So, in every family that I've stayed with, a discussion naturally grows as to who we are and where we are going; and believe me, much unrest suddenly appears within these homes, and this is often quite good. And as a stranger, but not as a zero, I can bring a certain good news to the scene, out of my own experience; for instance, I can talk to frightened husbands and wives about what I've seen happening in student communes—and the student communes are gradually growing into communes that include married people and families, as the students themselves grow. Then we can together seek and weigh such alternatives, the people in the particular family or group of families sheltering me.

Coles: What alternatives?

Berrigan: Well, in one situation I was close to last year, at Cornell, certain students had come together and bought land, and erected their own dwellings, and struggled through a very long winter, one which was especially cold and harsh. There were all kinds of people there—it was a settlement, I guess it can be called. There were ex-students. There were part-time students. There were people completely devoted to the scene: not working at all, except to cook or to clean or to do the tasks of the commune—and for the rest of their discipline they meditated, asked themselves why they were there and what life is about. So, many different kinds of people came together. In this particular commune were two married couples who had in fact been, with several others, the founders; I think they gave the commune a certain stability and maturity. Toward springtime they were all joined by a young woman who was a mother, but separated from her child's father, and she was welcomed. Now the presence of this little child seemed to make a great difference to everyone. People moved over, so to speak, to make suitable space for the child, and to find out what they could do for and be to the child; it was enchanting, really.

I learned a great deal in the time I spent there. The people demonstrated the parent in all of us; it seemed as though the infant was everyone's, and that parenthood mysteriously and gradually had come upon everyone there, so that everybody felt responsible for the child, everybody fondled the child, everybody spent time with the child. The child's happiness was evident, and the child's thriving physical state was evident. But what of the future? I think that commune is going to endure. I think that commune is going through something, is growing, is becoming something lasting—and hard to describe in words. For instance, they are all beginning to farm. They want to become self-sufficient. They want to discover what the land can do for them. And their relationship to the nearby town and to its politics is extraordinarily important. Some in the commune have been running a nonprofit bookstore and a restaurant in Collegetown for the college community; and in that way are keeping their relationship to their fellow students. In the store many students did more than buy books; there were poetry readings and musical events and all sorts of good things going on in that place of "business." You see, connections were being made; vibrations were going out; waves of feeling, expressions of concern and dedication. The commune wasn't utopian or cut-off.

Another aspect of the commune that I found exciting and promising was that the young people were "connecting" with, talking with, not only students but their farm neighbors, who in the beginning were quite suspicious and standoffish, and came looking around—I am sure because they wondered exactly what sort of criminal activity was going on. Instead those neighbors found a disarming simplicity and friendliness that the best of these young people are capable of. The result was that later, in the middle of the winter, the neighbors brought to the people in the commune bread and honey and cider and all sorts of things they were producing, and they stopped by to talk. Slowly these young people were accepted as neighbors, which I thought was very important. Well, all of that, I believe, gives us something to think about. I was touched and impressed by the attitudes toward property, and toward money and income, all of which were shared across the board. I was moved at the way art and music, literature and poetry, were woven unselfconsciously into the day-to-day living of the commune. When I would go out there for supper in the evening, we would end up with guitars and singing, and we would recite poetry —and all of that, I repeat, wasn't done in a phony, self-conscious, or pretentious way, but gently and naturally and spontaneously. They were not "marginal" people, not "dropouts," not possessed by negatives. They had a positive vision of things; they had alternatives to offer—something I take to be the hallmark of any significant movement, whether it be Catonsville or the commune. Well, as I say, one has these modest signs to offer.

Coles: Forgive me, but as one who has his own feeling of despair and who perhaps first believed in original sin, and now believes in the psychoanalytic version of it, which is that there are inevitably tensions and miseries and difficulties in all human relationships, I have to ask you this: what about the more somber or grim side of these communes? Or can it be that there is no such side, and that therefore my inclination to believe there *is* such a side constitutes evidence that I am captive of a certain kind of experience which I presumptuously insist upon as universally prevalent? In the same manner, perhaps, Freud, coming out of a middle class family and working with middle class neurotic patients in Vienna at the turn of the century, proceded to make general statements about human beings which may or may not be true of all human beings, but certainly people like me usually hold those psychoanalytic formulations to be true of all human beings, maybe because we are so damned parochial and entranced with our own knowledge, not to mention ourselves as the ones who possess that knowledge. Insofar as we psychiatrists have been interested in anthropology, we have begun at last to wonder about the universality of certain kinds of psychological qualities, and certain ways of growing up. But what about the communes? Do you see the kinds of rivalries and tensions that psychiatrists. say are inevitable in all human beings, are universal, and can never disappear?

Berrigan: I mentioned that commune because it is one of the very few I've experienced that has really succeeded, so I'm admittedly speaking of something rather limited. But in a sense that doesn't bother me—even if we have only one example we have a great deal to learn from it. I believe the commune survived, not only survived but flourished, because there were no severely troubled people involved. I think that has to be said. In other instances the communes have come together and broken up very rapidly because the people involved simply could not find common ground, could not find nonviolent ways of dealing with one another, and entered into the commune more or less as a way of solving something in their lives rather than primarily as a way of contributing something. This particular commune meant a great deal to me, and was uniquely strong, hence inspiring. And again: even one example in a bad time is a good thing. In that commune I think I discerned certain lines of understanding, certain styles of conduct, the sum of which drew individuals very much together. Now another group of friends of mine in a big metropolitan area have been meeting together for over a year now. They are people already professional men and women; they are in their late twenties, have children, and obviously are a contrast to the individuals I have just described to you. But as couples and families, they have begun to live together, not in the same dwelling, but in the same neighborhood. They are working out a number of problems. They are learning to share property—really to share their lives in a much deeper way than has been possible heretofore. They are joining together because they dread the violence they see everywhere, are horrified by the direction they see our various professions taking, and most of all, want to find something positive rather than react always to various negatives. I will watch their development with great interest—and hope.

Coles: What you describe is perhaps as radical as any political program can be—the reordering of lives along such lines.

Berrigan: I would think so.

Coles: I wonder whether the most radical challenge to the values in a particular society hasn't been made when families begin to reorder their living arrangements and the way they bring up their children. I suppose many of the people you've just talked about are thoroughly dissatisfied with things as they are; they apparently feel that it is not enough for a man to demonstrate generosity two or three hours a day, or read certain "progressive" or "liberal" publications with approval, or rail against *a* war or *a* particularly bothersome difficulty that the country is going through—but never make the kind of challenge to himself, professionally or personally, which would compel him to look beyond those few hours, and instead look at the core of his existence. I can think of nothing that would pull a person more into that inward kind of look, that scrutiny of a life and its assumptions, than a change in the way he or she lives from minute to minute, and day to day.

Berrigan: One thing I must mention: I find it especially important that everyone in the second group of people I referred to—the people in the urban situation—every single one of them is determined to be professionally responsible, no matter what changes they undertake in their personal lives. They all respect their background, their training; and they feel their lives *have* had meaning, even as they seek more meaning. They will not stop being doctors, lawyers, teachers. They want to have a further thrust, a longer reach. People who have been politically aware and active are also aware of the profound and unnecessary limitations our society presently places on their work, whether it has been in the inner city or whether it has been in the peace movement. And politically aware people hopefully become aware in other ways; they see that the problems they have as workers profoundly determine their so-called private lives. One cannot be exploited or thwarted from nine to five, then come home and feel loving and lovable. So it becomes almost inevitable that good people say: Look, it's good to be working at this job, or that job, it's good and important and in certain respects rewarding; but against the measure of what *might* be done, what might *be*, were things different, we can only feel driven to experiment, try different tacks, make changes in our lives. I remember one group of young professors and political activists who were talking along these lines and who undoubtedly will take a step this year in the direction of some sort of community, and it was very good to hear that they wanted to stay where they were, where their work was, but at the same time they wanted to undertake new experimentations in family life. I think they are all going to experience substantial tension, especially for the first year, as they try to reorder their lives. Necessarily they will have to come to terms with the question of children. How do such families, living together yet to a degree apart, bring up their children together? And then, how do the couples live close to other couples, yet also somewhat apart? The point is to hold on to the best of the past, yet gain a new sense of community, a sense of belonging to others, not just one's immediate self and spouse and children. It's almost a balancing act; it's an extraordinarily delicate thing to do, and a very difficult thing.

Coles: And in addition, of course, such people have to deal with their estrangement from the mainstream of the society, an estrangement which becomes increased as they move from isolated acts of political dissent to the far-reaching kind of disagreement that goes with living and bringing up children in ways thoroughly different from the ways that others in the society have been accustomed to calling their own. And I guess I wonder how this will be done, just as I wonder, say, how you manage personally to keep yourself from bitterness, from paranoia, from anger that consumes—because psychological "reactions" like those are occupational hazards, really, of taking on a struggle against a powerful foe, and not an "adversary" in the personal sense of the word, but an entire way of life, a whole society. Specifically, some two hundred million Americans live in certain respects similar lives; that is, they share certain beliefs, they get along in certain common ways. And those people have the police at their beck and call, and the army, and rewards or blandishments of one sort or another available. How does one deal with all of that, with the enormous pull and tug a society like ours exerts on all of us?

I asked myself that kind of question a few years ago, when I was living in the South and working with SNCC and CORE. It was easy to fight the segregationists and the sheriffs. Well, I don't mean easy; it was easi*er*, I believe, to fight them than to deal with other things: the notoriety, the public attention, the news stories and magazine articles, the sense of despair one gets as one fights and fights against an incredibly complicated and in many ways rather stable society, and last but not least, the criticisms of voices one carries within oneself almost as a cultural inheritance. Am I neurotic, one begins to wonder. Am I crazy for taking this stand? Why don't I settle down and "grow up"? Why don't I become a doctor or a lawyer, do something practical, do something that lasts longer than the time required for a particular sit-in or demonstration? In general what's the matter with me—not the nation, but *me!* Such voices are hard to shake off; and such voices so often summon a psychological language. Even though the young men and women I worked with knew what they were doing, knew they were in a sense asking questions that are the property, really, of a particular society—even so, those youths felt compelled to do so, to see themselves as others saw them. One of the things I could do, as a psychiatrist, was point out that some of these questions were questions which indicated how loyal they, as Americans, were to the very society they were protesting. Still, they struggled constantly with loneliness and weariness and the tension of taking on a powerful, persuasive, energetic, evangelistic society, all of which in many ways America is.

Berrigan: I think the things that you speak of—serious spiritual problems, the evidence of spiritual malaise—are exactly parallel to what the families I have mentioned are experiencing. They feel uneasy and dislocated as they take on the social system they belong to, but want changed; but they also still live with the feelings of doubt and emptiness and confusion which prompted them in the first place to experiment with new ways of living. It seems to me that the pain and anxiety and loneliness and bitterness you describe and I have seen in these unorthodox and innovative and activist people are all at least signs of an awakening. To grow one has to feel pain, know uneasiness—as you certainly must know from your work as a child psychiatrist. Isn't it more dangerous, more awful, when people *don't* feel the kinds of doubts and misgivings and confusions we've been talking about, when instead their voices are stifled by the permeating ideology, the official seductive presence of the state and the marketplace and the military machine? Is amnesia, is forgetfulness what you doctors call normal or desirable and healthy? How do psychiatrists recommend that young idealistic men and women deal with the grievous flaws in our society? Are those sensitive human beings only to make an incursion or two, an extracurricular advance here and there, against a culture of guns and conspicuous consumption? Must they eventually feel hopelessly captured by the worst in our national life, in spite of their own best instincts—feel that they cannot break free from what they have inherited?

Coles: I obviously cannot answer such questions. I am not as critical of this society as you are; I can feel myself rising to defend this nation, its traditions and values and hopes and even failures, as I listen to you. And yet, and yet; I mean, I wonder whether my "defense," as it swells up in me, doesn't satisfy you as evidence that I am deeply, maybe hopelessly caught up in the very web you have just described. And I suppose it is characteristic of people like me that we are always pointing out the problems and the difficulties and the tensions that we see in dissenters, while ignoring or forgetting or seriously understating the problems and difficulties and tensions (not to mention outright evils) those dissenters are struggling to break away from. It is obvious to us how troubled and disturbed many radical youth are, or how arrogant they appear to be, or violent. We are less inclined to notice how troubled and disturbed *we* are, the ones who do the name-calling; and how arrogant and even violent *we* are. What might be considered our arrogance, our meanness, our various flaws, to us simply comes across as "life"—and you would call all of that death: an inertia which allows for no real distance from oneself. Conrad's "the horror, the horror" was a truth about Western civilization—a truth which it seemed to take the distance of the middle of the jungle to enable. Presumably we don't, most of us, have that distance in our daily lives. Quite the contrary: we live surrounded by circumstances which we accept as simply the way things are. But given strong challenges to those sets of circumstances we so often become guarded indeed, and quick to attack those who trouble us, unsettle us, with their various assertions and challenges. And one way we defend ourselves and attack others is by saying things have to be the way they are (because it is the best of possible worlds); whereas (we insist) those who think things can markedly change are fatuous, utopian, blind, deluded—and on and on. So, a certain kind of despair may not only be a psychiatric symptom, but may be a way many of us have found to guard ourselves, ironically, against what psychiatrists claim they advocate: namely, a very realistic look at the world. We use despair in order not to see things. We become very cynical and critical of any possibility of change in order to protect ourselves from seeing just where we are.

2 • Pride and Violence

Coles: When one becomes a symbol one is tempted; the adulation and devotion someone like you gets from a number of people elevates you and puts you in a position of leadership but also, I would think, in a position which is dangerous and potentially corrupting.

Berrigan: Well, I reason that there is so much suffering in the world, so much injustice; and one must take risks to fight against injustice, and one risk, I would guess, is the risk that goes with taking an initiative—the risk you mention. It's awfully hard even to talk about this kind of thing. I am aware, I can sense the danger of it all—that one is accepted uncritically, worshiped almost, by people hungry for a kind of leadership they feel absent. But apart from the mistakes I make, or other people make in the way they look at me, what really matters is what is going on in the world, and what needs to be done to change things. The world is full of suffering and exploitation, and that fact keeps one in touch with the realities that make one's behavior a moral challenge. I've never had any difficulty in seeing that what I was doing was small in proportion to what other people were doing—people given "less" by fate and yet able to give so very much of themselves. I refer to the poor of this world who are fighting in one country after another for the right to own themselves, rather than be owned by others.

Coles: I agree; yet I ask you again about the sin of pride, something every leader, every innovator, every charismatic person presumably has to struggle with especially hard.

Berrigan: Well, I'm not clear about the form my sins take. (Is anyone, without God's help?) I do think that if the kind of pride you mention were a serious problem for me I would say so, and I would try to talk about it. At least I hope I would. But I have to say this: I am more worried by the children I have seen dying in Asia or Latin America or here at home among our poor than I am about my own pride—its degree or the forms it takes.

Coles: You keep mentioning what I suppose we call the "outside" or "objective" problems—which plague all continents and nations. How about violence and hate and exploitation in what is loosely called the movement? How about the brutishness one can presumably find in the underground, which is presumably made up of people who are escaping from what they conceive to be the violence of the society but which clearly has in it people who do not hesitate to use violence and endanger innocent lives. Pride, excessive self-assurance—they are the underpinnings of ideological arrogance, and so often the prelude to violence.

Berrigan: It seems to me that there are rhythms in everyone's life which require the kind of passive suffering that John of the Cross speaks about. When the Weatherman phenomenon was growing I had a choice of going forward with that development, and somehow making an adjustment and being at the side of the people who were preparing for violence and becoming less and less concerned with nonviolence. Or I had the option of standing aside, and I chose to do so because I couldn't accept that kind of approach, that violence. And I felt it important to tell those students going in the Weatherman direction what I felt, even if it meant they would no longer want to talk with me—which would be sad. I hope that one day sanity and compassion and community will assert themselves over all of us, the violence-prone in the movement and the violence-prone who run countries and order bombers to drop bombs and men to shoot at men.

Coles: Do you think that day is near at hand?

Berrigan: I am not so pessimistic about some of the students as I am about some of our politicians. I know some young people who have been Weathermen. They have gone through great personal anguish and tried hard to change this society, without much success, which they cannot forget. When they were picked up by the police they were not underground, but they were picked up in communes which they were forming for students and for working people and they were doing what the Panthers had been doing in New York City. They were with the people. They were dealing with students, especially high school students, and with the poor. Now they are in jail, and with very high sentences for what they did.

Coles: What did they do?

Berrigan: They were involved in trashing in Chicago, both at the convention and later when there were those other explosions going on, too; and as I said, that's all over with now because I believe they have undergone a change of attitude.

Coles: Then you feel that the law should not punish them for what they have done?

Berrigan: Let me speak personally. At this point the law is after me. I have never been able to look upon myself as a criminal and I would feel that in a society in which sanity is publicly available I could go on with the kind of work I have always done throughout my life. I never tried to hurt a person. I tried to do something symbolic with pieces of paper. We tend to overlook the crimes of our political and business leaders. We don't send to jail Presidents and their advisers and certain congressmen and senators who talk like bloodthirsty mass murderers. We concentrate obsessively and violently on people who are trying to say things very differently and operate in different ways.

Coles: How would you apply your thinking to those on the

political right who would like the same kind of immunity from prosecution and the same kind of right to stay out of jail in their underground?

Berrigan: Well, that subject came out very acutely at our trial; the judge and the prosecution essentially asked me the same question you just did. How would we feel about people invading our offices and burning our files? And our answer was a very simple thing: if that was done, the people who did it should also present their case before the public and before the judiciary and before the legal system and work it through and submit themselves to what we went through.

Coles: Well, how about one of the chiefs of the Klan who was arrested a while back and went through the process you describe—and as a result went to jail?

Berrigan: Yes, I think he is now in jail.

Coles: Would you argue that he perhaps should have taken to the underground?

Berrigan: Well, it seems to me what we have got to discover is whether nonviolence is an effective force for human change. The Klansmen, as I understand it, have been rather violent over the years; so their methods are not ours.

Coles: Are their methods any different from the Weathermen's methods?

Berrigan: Well, I look upon the Weathermen as a very different phenomenon because I have seen in them very different resources and purposes. I believe that their violent rhythm was induced by the violence of the society itself—and only after they struggled for a long time to be nonviolent. I don't think we can expect young people, passionate young people, to be indefinitely nonviolent when *every* pressure put on them is one of violence— which I think describes the insanity of our society. And I can excuse the violence of those people as a temporary thing. I don't see a hardened, long-term ideological violence operating, as in the case of the Klansmen.

Coles: You don't see that kind of purposeful and unremitting violence in the students?

Berrigan: Well, I am hopeful that the violence I do see in them will not take over and dominate them. I am going to continue to work—so that it doesn't happen.

Coles: This issue is a very important one, and I find it extremely difficult to deal with because—in my opinion and I'll say it—you're getting close to a position that Herbert Marcuse and others take: you feel that *you* have a right to decide what to "understand" and by implication be tolerant of, even approve, and what to condemn strongly or call "dangerous" at a given historical moment. You feel *you* have the right to judge what is a long-term ideological trend, and what isn't, and you also are judging one form of violence as temporary and perhaps cathartic and useful or certainly understandable, with the passions not necessarily being condoned, whereas another form of violence you rule out as automatically ideological. It isn't too long a step from that to a kind of elitism, if you'll forgive the expression— to an elitism that Marcuse exemplifies, in which he condones a self-elected group who have power and force behind them, who rule and outlaw others in the name of, presumably, the "better world" that they advocate. There is something there that I find very arrogant and self-righteous and dangerous.

Berrigan: Okay. Well, let's agree to differ on that, maybe from the point of view of a certain risk that I am willing to take in regard to those young people—a risk which I would be much less willing to take in regard to something as long-term and determined and formidable as the Klan. But I am willing to say that there is always danger in taking these risks, and that the only way in which I can keep free of that danger, reasonably free of it, is by saying in public and to myself that the Weatherman ideology (for instance) is going to meet up with people who are going to be very harshly and severely critical of it, as I have been and will be; in fact, at the point in which their rhetoric expresses disregard of human life and human dignity, I stand aside and I say *no,* as I will say no to the war machine. But I discern changes in our radical youth, including the Weathermen.

And again, I have hope for them, hope they will not be wedded to violence.

Coles: You feel they are no longer what they were?

Berrigan: Well, at least now there are divisions among them that are very significant, and with respect to the general agreement they have to remain underground and do underground work, there are very different reasons among them for doing that. Many of them have gone underground to work with the poor, rather than use dynamite.

Coles: They are not all of a piece?

Berrigan: Absolutely not.

Coles: They vary in many ways?

Berrigan: We simply cannot talk about just one stereotype of the Weathermen, or one kind of rejection of our society. I am going to try to work with them.

Coles: Work at communicating with them?

Berrigan: Right, and disagree with them thoroughly at times; because there is an absolutely crucial distinction between the burning down of property and the destroying of human lives.

Coles: You feel the courts and all of us as citizens should understand the distinction between the two?

Berrigan: Yes, and not only understand the distinction but embody it and gear their actions to that kind of distinction. This was acutely in my mind when I went to Catonsville. I wanted to emphasize how wantonly lives have been squandered in Asia—with no one punished for doing so; whereas we get stiff sentences for trying to highlight the tragedy by burning up government paper.

Coles: You mentioned a little while back that you especially have hope for our young who are university educated and who have their ideals if not their actions grounded in certain values that you share. I strongly disagree—in the sense that I have not found that people in universities (or, for that matter, many others who in this century have proclaimed the brotherhood of man) are any more immune to meanness and viciousness and snobbery than others of us are. Many of the people I work with (they are now called "middle Americans") are young people —and you don't talk about them, maybe don't know them. You mention young people often, but large numbers of young people are not going to universities, are not necessarily involved in politics, and may not be inspiring to people like you or me because they lack a political consciousness. But some of these young people may not be as murderous as some of the young people you're talking about. I think we've got to face squarely murderousness everywhere, even within our own ranks or among our colleagues or whatever. I can't be any more hopeful about some of the young Weathermen or some of the other young radicals than I am about the young, nonideological workers in this country, or for that matter the Southern whites I've worked with in the past. After all, one can say that in the past fifteen or twenty years Southern white people have gone through some very significant changes, and have responded in ways that neither they—nor to my knowledge many of the leaders in the civil rights movement—believed possible at the time (say 1960 or 1962 or 1963) the civil rights struggle was being waged in that region. (In 1962, I heard very tough members of SNCC and CORE say that *any* school desegregation in Mississippi was ten or fifteen years off!) I don't quite know how to put this clearly, but I get a feeling that sometimes we reserve for ourselves the right to ignore the most flagrant kinds of ideological rigidity, intellectual arrogance or meanness, and internecine warfare within our own cadres—then turn on others and criticize them for demonstrating similar qualities of mind and spirit. We deny others the kind of understanding and charity and compassion we ask for ourselves.

Berrigan: Well, I have no real difficulty with the kind of reservations you are expressing. It seems to me that practically everything we do or try to do produces a very tentative attitude among intellectual people—who worry and should worry about a lot of dangers and sins we are all prey to. I must say I am operating in our discussion out of a two-edged conviction that the university is the place where, ideally and even some-times in fact, humanity and human values are at least respected. I have no illusions about what happens in classrooms and what happens among academics—with their political jockeying for power and place. It all goes together—the valuable things in our universities and the ugliness, the essential ugliness of so much of that scene. But on the other hand I did see in three years, three very full years at Cornell, which was my last kind of ex-perience—I did see great things happening to certain members of that community, and I was one of the most savage critics of ninety percent of what was going on among students, faculty, and mostly the administration. So, despite my reservations, I do retain a conviction that the university is going to be a crucial proving ground for man's survival.

On the other hand I feel that the university scene is progres-sively condemning itself to death, and that the university as we have known it, just as the Church as we have known it, is not go-ing to survive. Even so, there is much that is important going on in both of those scenes—in our universities and our churches: people are pushing and shoving one another, and looking at themselves in new and honest ways. One finds so much surface there and so much rage, so much selfishness, and on the other hand, so much grandeur, so much real self-criti-cism. It seems to me that the university *should* be such a scene—because just as there are so many contradictions in American society, so one finds those contradictions on our campuses. There is no doubt, however, that having gone through the fif-ties, gone through the McCarthy era, we are now seeing anal-ogous dangers from the Left.

Well, you sense my ambivalence here. I was attracted to the university scene because I had a growing feeling that there I could learn in a kind of laboratory, a kind of hothouse labora-tory of human expression and human passion—I could learn what man might become or what he might refuse to become or how he might condemn himself to become nothing. And when I chose to live in a university setting I guess I lost touch, let's say, with working class people and their struggles, or the ghettos and their struggles, or the South and its struggle. But living in a university seemed very like the church scene so familiar to me—in the sense that a long tradition was in the throes of something very hard to define, something having to do with the struggle of life against death. But any scene of mixed life and death is extremely instructive in regard to the future, and is bound to be confusing and ambiguous and troublesome. I feel now as though I am being too abstract with you. Maybe I *do* tend to condone things, and need to be reminded of that; or maybe I *do* gloss over things because people I am instinctively or traditionally sympathetic to (rather than Klansmen) are doing them. The scene I'm in, like all scenes, I guess, is very skillful in concealing its own inherent ugliness, glossing over it with various self-justifications.

Coles: The radical scene?

Berrigan: Obviously, yes. What I am pleading for, what I continue to plead for, is that we see the reasons some of our radical youth have turned in the directions they recently have turned. To be very concrete, I have felt that the Weathermen phenomenon need never have occurred, and according to right reason should not have occurred, and in times which were less assailed by corrupt authority and corrupt power need not have occurred. The first instincts and the first tactics of these young people, at least in my experience of these young people, were not violent. They *became* violent. I ask why.

Coles: So you say our society has driven them to this?

Berrigan: That is the simplest way of putting it, and you know, we could be very concrete about this, and I could say that on the scene I knew, if there had been a different chronicle of events in the late nineteen sixties, the young people would not be so bitter and disillusioned.

Coles: You could say that about the Klan—that our society has driven them to do what they do.

Berrigan: Well then, all right, all right, and there again, let the Klan come forward and speak out its program, and let the Klan examine its own beginnings.

Coles: In the South one can hear the Klan doing precisely that all the time! Anyway, I don't mean just the Klan. I am trying to say that it is dangerous to say that people only do what society drives them to do. I am concerned with the issue of the individual's moral responsibility. I don't believe we are social automatons, at the mercy, always, of what politicians and other leaders decree. Then there is another question I'd like to ask you. How can a complicated society like American society, a large nation of many groups—how can it exist and stay reasonably intact and allow itself to be systematically undermined by any group that uses dynamite, that uses sustained violence and justifies that use? Now if you then say that every time this occurs one has to understand endlessly how the people in question got that way, came to do what they did—then where are we? Where are *you* as a theologian and *I* as a psychiatrist—where are we with these individuals; that is, where are we as citizens of a nation that has laws and a constitution which sanctions those laws? It is ironic that here the two of us are talking about people who presumably have a sense of *moral responsibility* and presumably feel themselves to have sensitive *consciences*. How can you and I, as people concerned with *individuals*, say that a given man or woman is only what society has made him or her to be? I don't quite agree with you. I think that the lives and deeds of some of the people we are talking about are not necessarily to be explained by what has been happening in America in the last three or four years. There is in some of their behavior, I think, a kind of petulance and meanness that I don't think I am ready to explain as only a function of the American political system. I think at some point we have to talk about *individuals*, we have to judge *individuals*—even as we ourselves have to be seen and maybe condemned for the individual choices we have made, or not made.

Berrigan: Yes, but at the same time I feel that our discussion is, at least so far, lopsided in its concentration upon the violence of a few who are out of power. We have not emphasized the violence of those who are *in* power. It seems to me that we, that *you*, are looking at the society as a kind of platonic entity which is self-justifying on principle and is functioning on behalf of individuals and for human life with a kind of structured compassion and justice and decency—and it is exactly those suppositions I take issue with. That is to say, the society itself is under judgment; I refer to its values, its deeds, its relationship to the international community, especially to the Third World. I feel that the best way to understand the violence and alienation of our young radicals is to look at America's violence, and America's alienation from the struggle of hundreds of millions of people for freedom from Western imperial rule.

Coles: Perhaps you should get more concrete.

Berrigan: Let me then offer an example, an example of the latent violence in our society which is taken for granted, which is simply woven into the fabric of our life—and the fabric is cut up into our habitual clothing, and we wear it, and it protects us. You no doubt remember the shocking outbreak by the black students at Cornell a year ago this spring. They seized a building; they left it with guns over their shoulders. The event became an international scandal of sorts, a source of horror among all good liberals, beginning with the *New York Times* and I suppose ending with the—I don't know what the corresponding papers are in Tokyo or West Germany. But that picture went around the world; those six or seven determined, angry young men coming out, marching out, with bandoliers over their shoulders and rifles in their hands. Their act was considered an attack upon everything the university stood for, upon all of its traditions, upon its willingness to allow minds free play and to accept differences of human opinion. As people, most people I am sure, looked upon that picture, they experienced shock and outrage; but perhaps they also experienced what Fanon has called "the first tremor in the white man, and the realization that his colony is no longer his." But apart from all

that, several significant facts were disregarded or played down
—for reasons I can only speculate about: number one, those
guns were not loaded; and number two, the bullets in the
bandoliers didn't fit the guns. And then I could go on to
say that the campus had always been armed, but the arms
around the campus for years and years had been in the hands
of the white middle class or wealthy students—in their fraternity houses. You could walk into one house after another and
see rifles on the walls. Furthermore, after the blacks entered
the building, it was surrounded by many white students, some
with weapons, and there were threats in the air that they would
enter the building and dispose of those blacks.

Now the university spent some fifty thousand dollars on a
detailed study of that whole episode, done by outsiders, at the
behest of the trustees. That report came out six or seven months
later, and was also widely publicized; it was actually published.
I studied the report very carefully, because obviously it was important. The university was trying to scrutinize a sudden, unprecedented, shocking, revolutionary action in its midst; was
also trying to understand the sources of social unrest and student
protest; and finally was in a sense fighting for its life. The report
came out toward the end of the summer and the returning
students had access to it. I was preaching at the university on
the opening Sunday in late September, and suddenly abandoned my sermon in favor of a commentary upon the report.
The closing paragraphs I'll try to summarize, because they were
at the heart of the matter. The reader was told that the university showed remarkable restraint in keeping the police at a distance, and in bargaining with the black students, thereby
preventing bloodshed; but at the same time the reader was told
that Cornell had chosen lives above property—and the question
to be pondered is whether or not such a choice is the desirable
one in the future. Period, end of report. Well, that and other
passages certainly offered me a great deal of material for my
attempted analysis, not merely of the blacks, but of the social
and political system out of which such an inhuman report

could emerge—and be considered "fair" or "thoughtful." We were being told that it is an open question, an arguable matter ethically, as to whether or not a building is or is not more important than the lives within it, the lives around it. I spoke of such a train of events as an incarnation of what I considered to be the colonial attitude; that is to say, Cornell's trustees consider the university their colony. They are the absentee owners of the place, so to speak. They share its life not at all; they come to it from outside, with their questionable virtues, so often (to be blunt) the virtue that goes with the possession of money—and much of that money commonly enabled by our Third World ventures, done at the expense of miserably poor natives. And it is those men who were determined to keep "law and order" at Cornell. Yet they could keep an "open mind" in a debate, triggered by the blacks, as to the relationship of life to property. Cannot one say that the blacks, by their threatened violence, exposed the violence and inhumanity in Cornell's trustees, and by extension in many who think similarly, and act similarly, too? Do you see what I mean?

Coles: I see what you mean, but I'm not at all sure that resort to violence is the best way to "expose" violence.

Berrigan: Most of all I want to point out that the report was received in utmost calm; indeed its message was not unwelcome to many professors, let alone the university's administrators. It seemed that only some students, some chaplains, and, of course, the blacks were seriously disturbed by the implications of the report. So, Cornell's institutionalized violence was revealed by the angry acts of black students—and white fraternity students; and the report more or less unwittingly offered a rather accurate blueprint of the prevailing attitudes of the university toward active dissenters and those who seriously and persistently question the status quo. When I preached that way, said essentially what I have just said to you, expressed solidarity with the sufferings and hopes of those black students and their white supporters, I received a letter of protest within three days from a vice-president of the university. He hadn't even been there to hear the sermon; he had read excerpts of the talk because it got into the news services. He scored me, because as he said—well, it went something like this: "At the beginning of the year when the university is trying to convey its return to peace, trying to welcome its new freshmen in a spirit of reconciliation and hope for the new year, you are deliberately muddying the waters again, by attacking the trustees of the university and this report." In other words, as far as I could translate it, he was advocating "peace at any price"—regardless of the violence which nevertheless persisted all over the campus, a kind of covert violence which keeps things as they are and becomes all too explicit when challenges to existing arrangements are launched. That vice-president of Cornell didn't want the kind of analysis I offered in the sermon—to a university audience, presumably entitled to its freedom of speech, freedom to hear what dissenters have to say. But perhaps this is too elaborate a kind of reflection upon what you were speaking of.

Coles: Well, I am unfamiliar with what went on at Cornell. I *am* familiar, however, with other instances of violence that go unrecorded as such. I am thinking of the violence I see in Appalachia or in migrant labor camps. When a coal company doesn't enforce safety standards in its mines, and an explosion occurs and men are killed, we read about an "accident," a "tragedy." We don't think of the *violence* done against those miners—by company officials bent on profits and government officials who go along with the companies rather than scream and shout and take action in courts and the Congress. By the same token when migrant workers are herded about like cattle all over the country and exposed to dangerous pesticides and paid miserable wages and housed in chicken coops and shacks flimsy and primitive beyond description, and when they get sick from contaminated water and food, and their children get sick and die because they live as they do and get no medical care— then we do not think to call growers *violent,* nor do we call derelict legislators *violent,* even though they have been unwilling to vote migrants the protective labor legislation they deserve as workers. And our universities until recently have traditionally signified for "honor" far fewer labor leaders than business leaders, have ignored men like Cesar Chavez in favor of generals and admirals. And universities all too often *selectively* insist that they stay distant from the "social issues" of the day. They involve themselves in one military contract after another—but worry that they will lose their "objectivity" or "neutrality" when they are urged to get involved in other causes or respond to the needs of people who are not working in the Pentagon and armed with billions of dollars.

In a way some of our students recently have been educating their college teachers and presidents, have supplied us with ethical leadership, have made it more difficult for boards of trustees to honor certain people with degrees, have made college trustees and presidents and administrators think twice about things they often never thought once about: namely, their expansion into communities, their relationship with surrounding populations. In that sense those students have reversed what one might think to be the usual order of things, in which older people serve as sources of moral inspiration for younger people. It seems to have worked quite in the other direction on many campuses, which may be a subject in and of itself; I mean, one can argue whether age and in this instance academic success necessarily bring with them wisdom, intelligence, discretion, and a higher order of knowledge and sensitivity.

Certainly when I was at Harvard as an undergraduate, I never questioned the fact that the university not only had its own police force, but was buying up property (and tearing down buildings) only in certain areas of Cambridge and not buying up property where the professors lived or where the wealthier people in Cambridge lived, but largely where poorer people lived. I never questioned that, I just thought it was part of the legitimate needs of a university—to have land, to put buildings on that land, so that people like me could learn. But I never asked, "Who am I? What people are being educated, and for what reason, by whom, and at whose expense?" Just as one, of course, often fails to ask oneself whose "law" and whose "order" is being upheld. In 1960, I watched four little black girls, citizens of the United States, residents of New Orleans, Louisiana, go into white schools. No one was shouting then about law and order. In fact, those girls were looked on as revolutionaries, they and their families. For trying to assert their rights as American citizens they were brutalized by mobs for months. Nor did they receive any support from the thousands of people in New Orleans who, I am sure, were embarrassed by the mobs—but not so embarrassed that they started asking what is *really* going on, what is *fundamentally* at work in Louisiana and other states as well.

3 • At the Edge

Berrigan: I have said that our society must be seen for the violent one it has been historically—and still is. My brother is in prison and I am a hunted felon—but men who plot war and shout racist obscenities are high officials of the federal government or governors or United States senators. The government pursues us just as it pursues its war—which means the government has certain all too consistent values some of us don't want to examine closely, lest we be made nervous or ashamed. To get to the real point: the supposition that society is a competent judge of its own members and of their activities—this is something that ought be subjected to the closest scrutiny and suspicion. It is up to good men to do so constantly. I simply can't say to you tonight that I believe that the government as presently constituted is fit to judge either me or the Klan or the Weathermen

Coles: But who is to decide whether the government is fit to make such judgments? Who decides whether the government is hopelessly corrupt and evil or simply a government, hence like all governments flawed somewhat. America is a nation, now two hundred years old; and it is this nation whose history in some ways haunts us. America has institutions and these institutions are givens, in the sense that we were born under a certain kind of government and in a certain nation, and we grew up to find out that this is our country. We can't reverse history—only try to make a different kind of history for our children to possess as their heritage. You are saying that our institutions are not fit institutions and therefore have no right to exercise their authority as institutions and determine, for instance, how to deal with violence, whether it be from the Klan or from the Weathermen. But if those institutions don't have such authority, *which* institutions, *which* people do?

Berrigan: We do.

Coles: Who is *we?*

Berrigan: Well, *we* are that small and assailed and powerless group of people who are nonviolent in principle and who are willing to suffer for our beliefs in the hope of creating something very different for those who will follow us. It is we who feel compelled to ask, along with, let's say, Bonhoeffer or Socrates or Jesus, how man is to live as a human being and how his communities are to form and to exist and to proliferate as instruments of human change and of human justice; and it is we who struggle to do more than pose the questions—but rather, live as though the questions were all-important, even though they cannot be immediately answered. My purpose in life is not to set up an alternative to the United States Government. We in the underground are trying to do something else. We want to say no to everything that is antihuman, and to suggest new ways for human beings to get on with each other. I believe from my own experience and from what I have seen happen to others that a new kind of life, a new way for people to live with one another, is quite possible—though I can't be as clear about the details of that life as you might wish, except to tell you at least this: I am trying to live now (to pay the price now of living) in a way that points to the future and indicates the directions I believe we must all take; and I can only hope that the future I speak of and work for and pray for will come about.

Coles: You are living out your present life in a way that you trust will make a difference to others yet unborn?

Berrigan: Yes, by living today as though the kind of tomorrow one prays for and dreams about is not completely unobtainable.

Coles: I'd like to get to a point that we almost reached just a while ago. I think you were saying or implying that people like me spend a lot of time discussing the violence of the radical left, or for that matter posing it as an issue comparable to the issue of the violence of the radical right, and at the same time— because of the kind of lives we live, because of the comforts and privileges we enjoy—do not dare to look at the institutionalized violence that is sometimes masked and veiled but is part of everyday life. Is that what you were saying or implying?

Berrigan: Well, the analogy I think that I am drawing upon is again the only one I know—the biblical experience of a man, Jesus. How does one really raise ethical and political questions and explore those questions in a real way—as contrasted to an academic or an intellectual way? Can someone question gross and blatant injustice from a life-situation that is tied in dozens of ways, often subtle ways, to that injustice? That is to say, it wouldn't have meant much to many of us if Jesus had raised questions of conscience and of God and man from the position of a Pharisee, from the dead center of his society. I can only mention a conviction, one I have tried to follow out, sometimes clumsily and incompletely—a conviction that one's position in relationship to a given society is terribly important, and bears constant watching. I find across the board that the position of clerics with regard to their ability and freedom to communicate (to be honest with themselves and others) resembles the position of lawyers or psychiatrists, or those in any other profession. We are finding that many people, young and older, find it unacceptable that a priest or minister make one religious pronouncement after another, and himself be immune from suffering or risk based on ethically inspired action; or that a lawyer talk endlessly about the law and its meaning and value and purpose—and himself do nothing to experience legal jeopardy in order to show the high crimes that poor and vulnerable people (from soldiers abroad to farm workers at home) experience at the hands of, yes, our lawmakers. My point is a very simple one: that we, as active and concerned individuals, are historically valid and useful for the future only in proportion as our lives are tasting some of the powerlessness which is the alternative to the wrong use of power today; and that's where I am.

Coles: At the edge.

Berrigan: At the edge. I suspect that in the traditional sense it is not necessarily a *religious* position, because all of these questions are very rapidly secularized. To put it very bluntly, the Jesuits of the sixteenth or seventeenth century lived underground in England to vindicate the unity of the Church. They were willing to do so rather than sit back and take no action to signify their sense of horror at the breakaway of England—an event which was to them a life and death question. And Jesuits have died to vindicate the truth of the Eucharist in other European countries. These were, of course, religious questions posed in a religious context. Protestants can speak in the same way about their martyrs. The difference now is, as a man like Bonhoeffer illustrated for us, that the questions are being posed across the board in a way that says: Shall man survive? Shall he weaken? Are you willing to live and to die in order that men might gain and win freedom, and not literally die in a holocaust or die the slow death that is the destiny of millions of the earth's poor? I can't conceive of myself as a Jesuit priest dying on behalf of the Eucharist, dying to vindicate the truth of the Eucharist, except in a very new way—except as the Eucharist would imply the fact that man is of value and that one does not kill and that one does not degrade and violate human life, and one is not a racist. Today, in other words, the important questions have an extraordinarily secularized kind of context. So I find myself at the side of the prophets or the martyrs, in however absurd and inferior a way, and I find no break with their tradition in what I am trying to stand for.

Coles: The Jesuits were politically underground and pursued by the police?

Berrigan: Oh, yes.

Coles: So you in that sense are going back to the order's history, the Jesuits' history?

Berrigan: Yes, that is true, and at the same time I am trying to transcend that history, because I think in one sense we cannot in these times go back to old ideological issues. In other words, I cannot pose in such a time as ours these questions as sacred questions, involving what I conceive to be a kind of Platonic dogma—even though I hope I believe as firmly in the reality of the Eucharist as seventeenth-century Jesuits did; and that belief is still very much at the center of my understanding of my life. For me to be underground because of my position and deeds with respect to the Vietnam war—well, I find in that predicament a continuity of spirit with what other Jesuits stood for. But I don't want to get away from something that you were raising here.

Coles: I raised the issue of how people like me deal with violence selectively, in the sense that we notice the explicit violence of the political radicals, be they at the Right or the Left, and are not so willing to be horrified by the everyday violence that our government either wages explicitly or in its own way permits, even sanctions, here at home.

Berrigan: Yes, or maybe more concretely and more nearly to our own lives, I think that we are, many of us, struggling for a new sense of what a professional life is—whether it be that of the cleric or that of the medical person or the teacher or the lawyer or whatever. It seems to me we have a revolutionary situation in which there is an increasing awareness that the structures which purportedly support and extend and protect human consciousness, human dignity, human life, are simply not working on behalf of man; and at that point, if that understanding is verifiable, if it's true, then it seems to me we are all in the same kettle of fish, and we each of us must move our professional life to the edge, so to speak, and begin again from the point of view of a shared jeopardy.

Coles: So you are asking how, for instance, a psychiatrist would do this. Well, you're not asking that. I suppose I have to ask it of myself—how I would move my life and my work nearer to the edge.

Berrigan: I was thinking about my own life: on the one hand I grew up in a certain way, and until ten years ago I had calmly accepted the idea that renewal of the clerical state had to do with a renewal of the energies that go with compassion and understanding and human diversity. I believed that to be a good cleric was to be more available, more understanding— some of the things that come through in your articles when you discuss your own profession. One was a good man in one's life if one's life was more and more available to others. I think that was right, that was sound—for the times. And then suddenly I began to realize something else which I still don't realize very well, but which I find verified again and again. I keep going back to Bonhoeffer and to my brother and to Martin King and to all those breakthroughs in consciousness which I have seen in people I respect, breakthroughs which had to do with something we really don't have a good word for. But I *can* describe something that binds the three men I have just mentioned and others like them all over the world: they have dared accept the political consequences of being human beings at a time when the fate of people, of the world, demanded that one not be merely a listener, or a good friend, but yes, be in trouble. So, in a way I can only be thankful that my life has edged over to the point that I am now simply, publicly, churchwise, society-wise an outsider, a troublemaker, a condemned man. I say that, I hope and pray, not to be arbitrary, or romantic, or self-serving in a dramatic way, but in order to respond to a reading of the times, as Bonhoeffer tried to read the times. And I am trying to draw analogies out of history, and other lives without being obsessive.

Coles: Or dogmatic.

Berrigan: Or dogmatic. One can be proven wrong; one can eventually find oneself mistaken. I will say to you that I would not be severely shaken tonight if suddenly, against all the evidence of the past years, I was to discover that I was on the wrong track. I would try to reverse that track, or get on another track; but I would also feel that it was more important to have explored this track than not to have. You know what I mean? To have entered into this present trouble with the law, to have entered into this anguish, to have entered into this separation from so many people I love—all of it has been necessary, I believe. Even if I were to reverse myself or as an act of conscience turn myself in and make an act of obeisance before the court, before the judge, and ask for mercy and go to jail; even if I were to go back on something I have started, I would still say, or I hope I would: go ahead and reverse yourself, but learn from what you did and why you did it. I would still remain convinced that in view of what goes on in the world, we must each of us explore and prod the world, and enter into *some* kind of jeopardy. I would still have severe trouble with America's political situation and its professions and its churches, and I would have to find another direction to make my misgivings *real*, to give them life through action. I could not remain at peace at the center, so the issue continues to be spatial—an issue of one's geography, one's place, one's decision to stand here, not there, and for this rather than for that. Where is one's heart and soul at work—for what cause, however humanly in error at times? Again, the issue is geographic.

Coles: You don't think that the problems you mention will always plague any kind of institution? Don't we always move from the radical critic or dissenter—be He Christ, be he Luther —to consolidations, institutional consolidations, then to a serious decline of the radical spirit with a parallel rise in cautiousness and institutional rigidity? I suppose you are saying that your reading of the times is such that we require a radical and active critique of our society, and of a kind we may not have needed at some other points in the history of this society. Is that what you would say? Or would you say that at *any* moment in *any* society the kind of radical position of jeopardy you spoke of has to be assumed by various people if that society is not automatically to go the way of, say, the Russian Revolution or the American Revolution or the Catholic Church, and indeed every political or religious or professional institution that ever was or will be? I am trying to distinguish between your statement about a particular moment of history in America today, and the problem you as a priest see afflicting your Church—a problem which certainly afflicts psychiatry and psychoanalysis a short thirty years after Freud's death, a problem which seems to rise inevitably once institutions become consolidated: they become cautious, inevitably dogmatic, exclusive, powerful, all too sure of themselves, abusive, rhetorical, and caricatures of the original intentions their founders had. Now how are we to distinguish between such a development in America, as a function of a nation's two hundred years of history, and the current emergency that you feel?

Berrigan: Well, I guess I could point to the fact that all kinds of people, people as diverse as nuclear experts like Oppenheimer and churchmen like Pope John, and spiritual leaders like Gandhi and Dr. King, expressed a common belief that the scientific revolution had introduced altogether new weapons against man, and new elements of jeopardy as far as human life is concerned. (We can all be killed, all two billion of us, in a matter of minutes.) It seems quite clear to me that we face something analogous to crises we've had before. But we also face something which we are justified in calling unique, and must deal with uniquely. I don't want to fall into a kind of smug, self-contented state—and when one says man has always had to deal with these problems one is close to that kind of state. I want to say, yes, we've always had these problems but at the same time there *is* a uniqueness to the threat posed by American power right now—posed in Vietnam, but also in other parts of Asia, and the Caribbean and Central America and South America. And I want to say as simply as I know how that I don't feel in my bones a responsibility toward the long stretches of history ahead. I'm not responsible for what is going to happen to my words or to my "followers" or to my Church or to my society in five hundred years. I believe that my concern has to be with the here-and-now; as a man and a Christian I feel bound to look about me, learn what is happening to human beings, and then respond to what I see and learn with the acts, the deeds of a brother. I do *not* believe that learning is enough. One learns, hopefully, to discover what is right, what needs to be righted— through work, through action. At some point one must take a position, actively or by default. One shares in and profits from the evils in a society, or one removes oneself enough to be at the edge, to take a sharply critical stand. What happens afterwards is the responsibility of the people who come after. Here and now I am responsible, it seems to me, for my time and energy. The question I have to ask myself every day is this: am I putting that time and energy into the quest I know is needed for a new and more decent way of living? I am sure that "way" will have its faults and weaknesses—but they will be the next generation's challenge.

Coles: Meanwhile, you have your responsibility as a particular human being alive at a particular moment in history.

Berrigan: Yes, and I believe I will be judged in accord with the attitudes I have shown, and the efforts in support of human life I have made, right here and now. I can only hope that what I do becomes part of what I guess can be called "the history of goodness."

Coles: You say that you feel American power uniquely dangerous to the world. I do not agree. I see American power as one element in the world, and one dangerous element. (Of course, all power is potentially dangerous.) But I do not see American power as *uniquely* dangerous—not when we have before us the spectacle of Soviet power, rising Chinese power, and falling British power. How can one overlook the murderous greed we have seen the Kremlin display? What is one to make of the outlandish iconography Mao's Peking unashamedly tried to impose on China, and maybe all Asia? Are Britain and France, with their hydrogen bombs, their waning but not dead imperialist ambitions, not a danger to many people in Asia and the Middle East and Africa?

Berrigan: De Gaulle once said something interesting which I don't think he followed very well. He said that since the great powers use violence as their method in the world it is not at all to be wondered at when the smaller powers, the lesser powers, follow suit. I think that was a sensible reading of things. And remember, we are the "greatest" of the great powers, so it is our example that others follow. But the real question is what one does to fight the nationalist violence this world still suffers from so grievously. I never expect decent activity from great power, whether it be church power or state power.

Coles: Or the professional power wielded by associations of professional men (the American Medical Association, the American Bar Association)?

Berrigan: Not from them, either. It seems to me that if we are thoughtful human beings we look at those secret beginnings and comings-together, those pioneering communities of men and women, which are very mysterious and are very hopeful and which symbolize, at least on the general landscape, man's goodness struggling for public expression.

Coles: Yet, you see those efforts (those social developments, one might call them) as always doomed by whatever political success they may enjoy—because such new beginnings (as Tillich would have called them), such hopeful expressions of freshness and honesty and openness are always subject to the corruption that seems to go along with success or power.

Berrigan: Yes, except that your word "always" is a very big word, and I am not sure history will bear out the necessity of using it. Sometimes I get the sense that in a way we are still part of man's prehistory, and we haven't the faintest inkling of what man can really turn out to be like—except through the example of some of the saints, some of the world's good men.

Meanwhile we may have to muck about almost in the same way primates mucked about before the "first man" appeared long ago—which is why I believe that word "always" on the whole scale of things may be improperly used. What I am getting at is that I don't accept the inevitability of, in a religious sense . . .

Coles: Of original sin?

Berrigan: Okay. Or let's say its omnipresent hold over human institutions.

Coles: You think man can be better than he has been in the past or appears to be now?

Berrigan: Well, I would put it like this: I think there has not yet been a real revolution. I think that whatever we *have* achieved has been extraordinarily partial (and as you suggest, tied to sin) and that there has not yet emerged a movement, a movement of people with the spiritual resources to explore systematically in every phase of its life nonviolence. The very fact that we have to use that word "nonviolence" I think reinforces what I am saying. There is no positive word for the kind of human conduct an expression like "nonviolence" only begins to suggest. We can't really put into words what we are struggling for.

Coles: Isn't Gandhi's word "satyagraha"—"truth-force"—a positive word or phrase?

Berrigan: Well, I can't quite find the words for what I am trying to reach toward. But in general with regard to the movement it seems to me quite clear that I have to use expressions like nonviolence and I am dissatisfied with them because I think that we're on the shadowy side of something which we haven't stepped into yet. To push this thing further, I believe that it is entirely possible that the first instance of a really great breakthrough is going to take place in America. I say that because I think this war has really forced a lot of people to stop and think about all sorts of things—to the point that they may never again be the same, those people.

Coles: You feel optimistic about the possibilities in individuals, and by that I mean the radical possibilities. You feel we

can significantly transcend what others have called our "fini-
tude," our psychological and spiritual limitations as human beings—limitations which have plagued even the best intentioned,
throughout history.

Berrigan: What would you think of an example like this?
About a year and a half ago, after Catonsville for sure, I was
involved in a retreat. We were gathered together, about thirty
people—clerics and movement young people, students, activists
—and we were discussing, because they wanted to discuss it, the
direction of things after Catonsville, and where their lives might
intercept with that direction. Someone told me in confidence
during the retreat that present among us was a girl who was
seriously contemplating self-immolation. The girl was just com-
pleting on this retreat a forty-day fast; she had taken only a
little water for that period. I was asked whether I would try in
whatever way I could to talk with her, because she had come
wanting to talk but she couldn't quite make the first overture.
And so I did. I went walking with this girl, and she began to
talk to me. It appeared that she had been in the movement for
two or three years, had been brutalized by a very harsh jail experience—and yet she was filled with joy. That was what
struck me, as I tried to understand and discuss things with her.
After a period of time she mentioned that she felt there was a
further gift to be offered—and that was the way she brought up
the subject of self-immolation. Well, what I was looking for in
her were signs of despair, signs of fear, signs of enough hopelessness to drive her over the edge, signs that she had lost her
sense of herself. And yet I couldn't find those signs in her.

Coles: You said you found joy?

Berrigan: Yes, I found the kind of joy that expressed itself in a
remark she made: "I've done everything I know how so far and
nothing has changed. Maybe a further act of mine will affect
people; maybe if I show I want to give my life itself in this way,
they will stop and think about *their* lives, this *country's* life."
Even so, I continued to wonder whether this young person was
not deeply troubled. Try as I might, though, I couldn't find any-

thing but wholeness in her. Finally I said this to her: Suppose you were to find a community in which people were trying to go forward to something like we did at Catonsville, a community dedicated to nonviolence, a community (however marginal) whose members shared the anguish you feel. Would you join them and would you go forward with their discussions and their explorations and at least put off this plan you're now considering? She said she would—and she did. I've lost contact with her but I am quite sure she has not immolated herself and has instead found that she can go forward with a certain group of young people.

Now why did I mention that girl in this context? I'm always searching for signs out of lives like hers that will help me to understand the limits of hope and the meaning of communities at the edge. I thought that I helped to lead her to such a community—a community which would free her of the need for that kind of ultimate expression. Obviously I was in great suffering about her contemplated action; I was convinced that it was neither necessary nor desirable.

You know, one remembers such a young person; she becomes a sign for one's own life, a sign of what one can help others toward. Before I met that young lady I knew a young man who immolated himself out of what we could only agree was despair, and then another man, a Quaker, immolated himself at the Pentagon and my friends and my brother especially—he knew the man better than I—were convinced that he immolated himself as an act of hope.

Coles: So you do not look upon these people as necessarily deranged or disturbed?

Berrigan: No, not necessarily. In certain instances no, in other instances yes. I was at the bedside of a boy in Syracuse who immolated himself in front of a cathedral there—it was Easter of sixty-eight I guess—and I had been to Hanoi and I had seen what our bombs do, what our antipersonnel weaponry was doing to civilians, to children and their parents, and then I came home and this boy burned himself and he lived for a long time. I was compelled to go over and search him out, visit him. I got in because I was a cleric, even though he was in an isolation ward, receiving special care. I leaned over his bedside and I smelled what I had smelled in Hanoi—burned flesh. I then talked with him; and as far as I was able to piece things together his act was an act of hope; so he quietly and thoughtfully construed it. He was an honors student, a high school senior who was not wild or overly good; "just sensitive," people said.

4 • Compassionate Man and Political Man

Berrigan: Perhaps we could now discuss the distinction between the "man of compassion" and the "political man." It is a distinction a man like me begins to comprehend when he contrasts in his mind a ministry to the Church, and a ministry of the Church to the world. And it is a distinction which has to do with the "passage of soul" my brother and I have undergone. We really entered into a radical stance with regard to society when we understood the connection between political action, responsible political action, and the Gospel itself. We began to see that what mattered to us was not that the Church serve herself, and not that ministers of the Church continually look upon their lives as based upon private prayer and public dedication to those who belong within the "household of faith," so to speak; but rather that the Church more than anything else try to be a sign to the world, a sign that goes beyond itself, as any sign obviously does or should do. Especially in this culture the Church has become almost irredeemably bureaucratic and self-interested and self-regarding. For example, the ideal bishop is thought to be a man who keeps house, a man who is a builder and a financier, a man who knows how to accumulate and deal with "power." The

Catholic bishops, at least, have stood so far within the center of their own possessions, and have (it seems to me) become so profoundly secularized that they were simply unequipped to understand the war in Vietnam as a moral question. It is hard to say this, but I believe for many bishops there is nothing in their daily lives that a man upset by war and racism can appeal to. Thus do men of the Church get cut off from the Gospel—and come to serve their Caesars. So for moral leadership one turns elsewhere—outside the institutional Church. I suppose we had to turn backwards, to the Church's very beginnings. The day Phil and I decided that we had to say no to the war, in however clumsy and inept a way, we were simply reasserting something very close to the Church's beginnings; as Bonhoeffer said, "Jesus was a man for others," and those "others" are, in fact, mankind.

Coles: The Church's predicament may be comparable to the predicament of institutional psychiatry, or for that matter many other professions. You remark upon the moral failure of the Church, which is presumably meant to be, if nothing else, a *moral force;* by the same token in my profession many psychiatrists and psychoanalysts (whose *job it is* to find out what happens to children growing up) have been unwilling to look at the way a child's "position" in society (his or her class, his race, his "background") affects the way he or she is brought up. Doctors who spend their lives trying to understand the human mind can somehow enable themselves *not* to look at how a child becomes systematically indoctrinated into a given set of political assumptions, how a child learns to go along with a particular kind of social system, learns not only to obey the law, but learns to hate or distrust certain people, even at times to lose all sense of compassion or sensitivity with respect to those "different" in this or that respect from himself or herself. In other words, the systematic study we claim to make of the human mind is a systematic study that is much more limited than we often care to acknowledge. We study certain things; we *don't* study other things. So I think that just as there is a certain moral lethargy or worse in certain quarters of the Church, which is an irony because the

Church if anything is presumably a moral institution, so there are psychological inhibitions among psychiatrists, who presumably feel themselves of all people the ones best able to examine and undo psychological inhibitions. Do you follow the line of reasoning?

Berrigan: Yes.

Coles: It's not an exact analogy.

Berrigan: I'm wondering whether or not it's useful to suggest that both churchmen and professional men—if they are to stay alive as persons—need constantly to cross the borders, the boundaries, they so often establish for themselves. When I was in Hanoi I felt to a certain extent excluded from the people there; they were in the midst of great ferment and struggle. Yet because I went there I came back to this country more aware of so many things. I'm not just talking about the advantages of travel. I believe I crossed more than great distances and certain national borders or boundaries when I went to Hanoi. And I remember in 1965 I had trouble getting to Eastern Europe and Russia; at that time it was still practically unheard of for a Western priest to go there, and I was received with great suspicion —even as I was only reluctantly allowed to go. Yet, I learned so very much—and maybe more important, unlearned so very much. We get so self-centered in our beliefs and attitudes. We are condemned by our national and ethnic and regional and racial ties. So, it is important for churchmen to go to Hanoi as brothers of those under fire and as enemies of no one—so as to reassert the fact that Christ's faith is universal, and that He doesn't recognize the lines drawn in the soil by mutual military establishments. And by the way, how important it would be for psychiatrists also to go to Hanoi—and study firsthand the consciousness of a stubborn people fighting against such great odds. How do such people survive, and what within them allows them to keep their hope and to keep their gentleness, to keep their communities operating under the most murderous of conditions?

Coles: One might ask the same question about certain people in this country—people who are putting themselves in positions of great jeopardy. What enables those people to keep themselves going, despite all the harassments and penalties they face?

Berrigan: I'm groping toward something that I think began to come to me around five years ago, back in '65. Then I was surrounded in Paris with so much of everything I had known at home. I was missing something without being able to define it. I now realize that my spirit was simply dying. I craved escape from a self-congratulatory life—a life with few if any challenges. It was very important for me to go see Africa and Eastern Europe and Russia at that time. I was isolated, extraordinarily isolated. Similarly, nations can become smug and isolated. We were isolated in one way in the 1930s, and in another way during the 1950s and 1960s, when we became "internationalist"—but often not in order to understand other peoples but keep them under our control. Many Americans know less and less about worlds other than their own; hence they are progressively less and less able to assess their place within their own society. Now, you ask how one can fight such a situation—and keep his cool. Well, I ask you: how can one *not* fight such a situation and stay even half alive in mind and spirit? By the same token there must be Russians who are faced with the same dilemma, because their leaders have certainly shown themselves to be as thoughtless and violent as some of ours have been. I think we're at the point where everything going on in the world leads us to the conclusion that unless man becomes universal man (and not nationalistic man) he is going to be amputated man, in a spiritual sense.

Coles: If indeed we survive at all.

Berrigan: One can survive in body but be dead in spirit— which means, selfish, exploitative, filled with self-serving slogans. One can be warthirsty, or greedy for more power over more people—and so be the Devil, if not physically dead. And amid all the wars we have had during this century, the myth persists that decent men can remain decent and compassionate, and still profit from the spoils of war. It is as if we delude ourselves into thinking that we can have our spiritual and psychological butter, and still wield those guns, which kill people.

Coles: I suppose we believe that as individuals we are immune to the dangers you mention.

Berrigan: Or that we will remain undamaged by the poisonous atmosphere about us. And so it goes: intellectuals betray themselves and others, and priests betray Christ. I don't think that people in this country by and large are aware that the choices are being constantly narrowed as to how one can live one's life and how one can do one's work. The Bill of Rights means less and less. Men are spied upon more and more—even prominent and not particularly controversial men. As for priests, the choices for them are certainly limited, and painfully so if they are aware human beings who want to have some significant part in a community of believers, to lead them maybe, or not necessarily to lead them, but show personally and in public on behalf of them a sign of concern, a sign that is inspired by Christ's example, a sign that can be read as saying: "I am for others, I am here and now for others."

Coles: Let me ask you how you would reply to the argument Bernanos puts forth in *The Diary of a Country Priest*—that all a priest can do is try to be the priest of the individual parishioner, and that insofar as the priest moves away from that hard task he is succumbing to a variety of temptations and errors, if not sins. Similarly, what the psychiatrist says, or the lawyer says, is that the world is full of particular individuals who need help of one kind or another—and to offer that help is all a doctor or lawyer, *as* a doctor, *as* a lawyer, can do. But you say, I believe, that to be a "compassionate man" is not enough. You ask that one become a "political man" who takes stands on the larger issues, and does so not in spare time but wholeheartedly and perhaps in a full-time way. Meanwhile individuals continue to have their daily troubles, and require devoted help from doctors or lawyers. In any event, is it in your mind quite suitable for a priest to be *only* the padre, the curé, the "man of the cloth," the man who listens to confessions, helps particular families get through this life as best they can? Or is such a position now untenable so far as you are concerned?

Berrigan: Well, could I just step back a bit on that question? I think it is an important one, and a very vexing one, an extraordinarily difficult one. What is the priest's essential task? That is what we're trying to ask. First of all, it seems to me, Bernanos sets up (within a given cultural situation) a magnificent and traditional example of the priest—and when I use the word traditional, I mean it in a noble sense. Bernanos's priest is close to the heart of our faith. He understands that and can embody that. Bernanos places the man, the priest, in the midst of the French landscape in a way that is very moving and attractive and authentic—and I begin by saying that. But I think we have to move from such a life to the kind of living we in America now face. We simply cannot romanticize that figure, who belonged to nineteenth-century rural France. I must ask myself: what is the essence of that priest's virtue, and how can that essence be spiritually transplanted into the sour and bitter and rocky soil that twentieth-century America possesses—no easy job to do. And yet, if I may immediately contradict myself, I find it very simple to do, because I think the moral power of that priest of Bernanos's—he has stayed with me for a period of fifteen or twenty years now, and has meant so much to me— lives on among many of the Catholics I have been working with in recent years. In other words, I would try to get at the essence of Bernanos's curate in this way: he speaks to me of the fact that without a contemplative side, without sacramental experience, one is nothing as a priest, and one has nothing to give. Who can forget that curate—no matter how different his life was, and no matter what one's own experience has amounted to, be it in prison or out on the streets as a political activist? Against a figure like that, I can also judge the frivolities and idiocies and the betrayals of some priests in America, who after a while are floating free in the culture, with nothing to give it, no critique upon it, no "no" to say to it—and how sad for them, for all of us. Again, we hopefully will never lose what the curate offers us, because to lose that is to lose a kind of living access to Jesus Himself; and that is the way I would look upon it, you know: the example of a saint is a very sacramental thing. As for the fact that the curate is not political, I would certainly not want to criticize the novel or the curate on that count. The curate is what he is within a given ambiance; and yet at the same time one ought not make the novel a universal recipe for the priesthood today. I think that such a novel presents us with very subtle nuances which only with great difficulty can be translated into our own lives, and become genuinely a part of us— rather than imported or airlifted in from the outside as a Platonic ideal, something one ought not try to do with Jesus, either.

Coles: You are warning against the temptation to use a nineteenth-century figure (or a first-century figure!) as a means of not facing the concrete and difficult problems we have in the twentieth century. If we do so with the curate, use him for our own devious and nostalgic purposes, we are terribly unfair to Bernanos.

Berrigan: What lives in that novel lives, by analogy, in the historical Christ. After all, two thousand years ago there appeared in a little occupied state of the Near East a wandering rabbi. I suppose at the time many people thought Him and His followers quite "provincial," but from the point of view of the spirit a floodgate was opened and the result is still felt by us. Thus does a life pass into history, thereby to nourish the living at every point in which their lives are threatened and in danger of suffocation. And Christ's "grace" is now available to us, not in order that we become historical outcasts, or strangers to our own times, but to make us more firmly at home with those around us who need our exertions—and to put us near that particular grind of machinery that we are destined to hear with our ears. There obviously is no one pattern for any life, or for any community of lives; in fact, I think the mark of a community's vitality is the variety of expressions its tradition allows.

But to go back to the curé for a moment: for years I have been meeting all kinds of American priests, and I think I can understand their—our—agony. Many of the priests I have met I would call "little curés" in their sensibility; that is to say, their compassion operates in a very direct way with a relatively small number of people. Such priests have always been a great inspiration to me. In no way do I want to challenge them—or urge them to be different. What I *do* find sad is something else. I refer to the priests I have met—alas, so many of them—who are dissatisfied with the Church because they have never really discovered the Church. Such priests often contemplate or actually take steps to leave the ministry, usually by way of marriage. But all too often their passage from the Church into the larger American culture is the passage of a water bug or a butterfly —a successive touching of the surface of things. The passage outward really solves nothing; they feel themselves as thwarted in the world as they did in the Church. They have moved from what I would call a rather compliant and inert Church to a culture which is in fact the outer mold of that Church.

Coles: So there is no escaping.

Berrigan: For *them.*

Coles: Or, I suppose, for anyone unless there is a radical transformation within the person that enables him to see some of the things you have pointed out. The continuity between whatever it is that those priests want to escape from and whatever it is they want to escape to—isn't that the problem you're insisting upon?

Berrigan: It's a very very difficult matter—and I'm sure it's also difficult in different but also similar ways for Protestant ministers. It's so very hard to find a way of living out a life of faith, as the Gospel invites us to do, because our American culture is so torn yet so persuasive, and also so blind to its own inner workings, its own values and lack of values.

Coles: Do you think all cultures are like that?

Berrigan: Well, I think it's a difficult thing today to find a culture that is convincingly on the side of human life, and lucid about its own ethical position—and so not victimized by its own rhetoric. And how hard it is, correspondingly, for each of us to say, "I am this" or "I am not that" and be in touch with the facts as they are. Well, maybe that is taking us afield.

5 • Professional Life

Berrigan: I'd like to ask *you* some questions—I mean, ask what issues you believe your profession ought to be struggling with in times like these. Do you think a professional man like yourself is free to inquire broadly, free to do and say whatever he believes right and proper?

Coles: I fear that all too many psychiatrists and lawyers and teachers and architects in New Orleans or in Boston or Seattle manage quite successfully to come to terms with the powers that be, and never once start asking themselves what assumptions they have to make every day about the structure of the world around them, where their money comes from, who pays them, who rewards them, whom they *don't* see as patients or clients, whom they never get to represent—who cannot purchase their time. I remember one day when I was taking my residency training in psychiatry I heard a supervisor of mine say, "We are in the business of selling time to people." Because I fancied myself somewhat idealistic, that seemed like a rather crude way of putting things, so I turned upon him in my mind, and said to myself (not him, because I wanted to get through and be awarded my certificate!), "What a vulgar man, to think of a psychiatrist as one who sells his time to people." I thought of myself as sincere and generous and anxious to give my time to anyone who came to me, so that we could all help one another grow as individuals. But more recently I have thought back upon that moment, and now I'm not so sure the doctor wasn't right in coming out with that kind of almost vulgar confrontation—which in turn compelled me to look at certain brute facts, and stripped away from my mind one might say an almost fraudulent idealism. The facts are that I *do* sell my time, or if I personally do not, most people like me do. We sell our time to people who can afford to pay thirty or forty dollars an hour for it. In that sense, of course, some of the confrontations now going on in our society may have a liberating effect on the society. The obscenity, the pornography, the greed, the self-aggrandizement, the parochialism that are protected and considered to be part of everyday life, are being confronted—and the result is a great deal of outrage on the part of people like me, who don't want to think of ourselves as "up for sale," as "purchased at a going rate" by a certain class of people, but who rather have been accustomed to think of ourselves as noble and idealistic and decent and honorable. No wonder we squeal with pain or, for that matter, turn on people who would compel of us moments of self-analysis as well as social or political analysis.

Berrigan: Why is it that there are no psychiatrists in jail at this point in American history?

Coles: I think your question is interesting indeed—in view of the fact that we are secular moral leaders of sorts, called upon for advice about anything and everything by anyone and everyone; and in view of the fact that so many people ask us for opinions about all kinds of ethical issues, about how to bring up children, about what is right and what is wrong, what is sane and what is insane, what is "good" and what is "bad" for the "person," for the "personality," for the family. Even more to the point is what do psychiatrists think of those who *are* in jail or who take stands which the federal or state authorities want to punish with jail sentences? What do they say about

Dr. King or Dr. Levy or Dr. Spock or Cesar Chavez? Do they call such men "immature"? Do they say that in some way those men are "acting out a neurotic problem"? Many of us, and not only doctors, do just that, think in just that way. We think of people who are taking up one or another eccentric position in relationship to our society as troubled people who need help, who need "treatment," who need to be analyzed, who need to be looked at, who need to get rid of their "problems," so that, presumably, they will be better "adjusted," more "normal"— and the words go on and on, and reveal how both we here (and needless to say, in a much worse way the Soviets) have found a certain kind of psychiatric nomenclature all too convenient. Then of course there are those psychiatrists who say that their profession has no values, that they are only interested in "understanding," in "learning." But of course, having said that, they don't usually try to *understand*, to *learn*, why it is that they see one set of patients rather than another, and what effect such a practice has on their view of the nature of the mind.

I have to keep on emphasizing that we psychiatrists are, like members of any profession, part of a given society, and very much attached to it; and the nature of that society affects our assumptions, the way we look at people, and the conclusions we come to about people, which is particularly painful and ironic in our case, because so many of us talk about being "scientific," which is supposed to mean "objective" and "value free." I have to mention again and again that during the sixties in the South I saw psychiatrists used by the courts in order to pin labels on protesters, confine them, judge them. One youthful dissenter after another was sent to a mental hospital for evaluation, and the courts considered such an approach "more humanistic": a person would go to a hospital, rather than to jail. Certainly the violent response of the segregationist "law" which dominated the state courts of the South could in that way be somewhat masked or made less obvious. But I am being evasive. I can't presume to answer your blunt question for other psychiatrists. I can only say that I am one psychiatrist who doesn't want to go against the laws of this country and would be afraid to go to jail.

Berrigan: Would you allow for the possibility that there was something important going on in the minds of those students, something extraordinarily significant for professional men to look at?

Coles: Yes. And I'm afraid it's something that, as a psychiatrist, I'm ill equipped to comprehend—and you can see it in the tenor of the questions I've been putting to you. I am equipped to comprehend deviance, disorder, rivalry, tension, animosity, belligerence, truculence, nastiness; not only am I prepared to comprehend such things, I in fact manage to see them everywhere. And if I don't see what I'm looking for, I ask why and look harder and eventually to my own satisfaction succeed in what is a quest of sorts, I suppose. If I am thwarted, I can always say that the person who is not displaying this or that to me is extremely well-guarded or "defended," and that itself is a sign of the difficulty I'm looking for. So, one way or another I'm going to find what confirms my way of looking at the world. And my way of looking at the world is, again, to see the *problems* people have, the struggles they go through, the sly and devious mental maneuvers they put themselves (and others) through. In a sense I see a jungle everywhere, in everyone's mind: "It's still the same old story, a fight for love and glory," to quote from the song in *Casablanca.* Now there *is* that struggle—and not for a moment should we whistle in the dark and deny how difficult and mean and self-centered and grasping people can be, *children* can be, even *before* they go to school. But by the same token we are also many other things—capable of decency and honor and kindness and generosity, capable of sharing solidarity with those less fortunate, capable of being in our own small ways like Bonhoeffer. We psychiatrists are often less interested in "studying" that side of "human nature"; our training often ill equips us even to look for that side, nor do we often enough ask ourselves what price both we and our patients pay for such a psychiatric "philosophy" of the mind. Instead we try to help our patients "live within the world they're a part of." I heard that phrase over and over again when I was in training. I wonder why we weren't encouraged at least to discuss other possibilities—consider whether both we and our patients didn't have more of a responsibility to be skeptical, uncompliant, and in some spheres thoroughly angry and rebellious.

Berrigan: It seems to me that you have been mentioning issues anyone who has undergone professional preparation of any kind ought to worry about—but too many don't even stop and think about. As bad as things were for us when we "prepared" ourselves to be doctors or lawyers or architects or teachers or priests, and as much as we felt ourselves being stifled and made all too obliging and conforming—still, we acquired skills, and the challenge now is to use those skills for purposes that are important, to share those skills with those who need them and have no access to them. I could express as deeply as you have my dissatisfaction with my seminary training. At the same time, I can only say that the task now is to move forward— and not get bogged down in the sadness and regret we feel about the past: the opportunities lost, the difficulties experienced. You have moved on to your own work, and I hope I have done so, too. What we both can tell one another about our respective periods of "training" comes down to this: professional education in America, maybe everywhere, is both valuable and dangerous—because one acquires important tools, but one has to fight hard to stay loyal to one's values, to stay spiritually alive. That training at least gives one the ability to *do* something, and also gives one a certain world view, a certain limited but important competence; but that training must now itself be submitted to scrutiny and evaluation and examination, even as thousands and thousands of medical students and law students and seminarians went through quizzes and tests to prove themselves. I mean, the professions must ask themselves if they are responding to the needs of people for medical care or legal assistance or spiritual energy—rather than giving them a hypnotically pacifying ritual. Nor can one at any point in his training, or at any point after his training is done, feel that he is securely prepared for what is ahead. I said to myself last June: Well, I've been in my order thirty years now, and I've been an ordained priest for about eighteen years, and I know that I have had to change more in the last five years than I had to change in the preceding thirty, and I know in my heart (though I dread saying it even to myself) that I am going to have to change more in the next year than I have in the last five. I know such is going to be the case in the future, too—so the best I can do is say, in however shrinking and terrified a way: all right, that's the way it will be, and I will do my best. Nor do I believe I am alone. I think all of us are caught up in the tremendous changes now going on, and we simply cannot fall back on the degrees we once obtained, the credentials we have, the certificates we have hanging on our walls.

I believe the priesthood is self-creating or self-destroying, almost like one of those new artists' pieces of machinery—machinery which sort of light up and move around and collapse, or suddenly undergo some sort of internal transformation into something else. I think that by and large the professions, all of them, share a common assumption, one which I would like to attack. You have brought it up certainly—the assumption; it is that we are as professional men a sum, the sum of those energies and talents and achievements we have managed to amass during our long period of training and our "rise" to positions of status and respectability. After we get there no one ought question us—because that "sum" is static and unassailable, so many dollars of performance and distinction and worth. So, we get tenure at a university, or in the instance of the Jesuits we get our degrees and our places of honor in the religious community, or with doctors we get our appointments on hospital staffs— and at that point we begin to level off, as far as our growth goes. We have only to ride the wave that has developed on our behalf as professionals or as churchmen, as if at a certain point a halt is called to our growth; childhood and adolescence may well be explosive and chaotic and fiery, but adulthood must be characterized by a certain kind of static achievement, with a consequent undertow. One becomes turned into statuary, turned into a prestigious figure who cannot be seriously questioned. I think that everything in life ought to be open to discussion and criticism—and it is sometimes absurdly selfish for those of us who have "arrived" to stop asking ourselves *how* we arrived and at what price. Nor should we choke off others, young or old, who want to ask the same questions.

Coles: Let me interrupt you to agree that the struggles you have just mentioned—between critics of one sort or another and established professors or religious leaders—plague all professions. When young psychiatrists in training start to question their teachers too strenuously or speak too critically of theories sometimes handed down to them like laws or articles of religious faith, they can be called "troubled," be told that they need "more analysis," be asked what their "problem" is that prompts such radical doubt. So ideological postures, professional self-righteousness, power politics, the exploitation of the weak or the aspiring by the strong and self-satisfied—all of that, to me, is universal, the result of man's capacity for harm, his egoism, his drives and lusts as they become expressed institutionally. Particularly sad is the way the weak young man (the young doctor or teacher or lawyer or priest) on the rise, on the make, feels compelled to turn upon himself after any rebellious moments he may experience. In order to graduate and be declared certified and authorized and approved, the young man in his own mind becomes a sinner—faulted, troubled, in need of help, in need of a change of "attitude." In the twentieth century, in the name of science and honesty, professional men (presumably by and large agnostic and with an image of themselves as generous and liberal) can persecute one another, can be vicious toward one another, can be vindictive and narrow-minded and intolerant. So cadres of young "trainees" meet up with rigid and doctrinaire teachers who have this message for all who come to learn: conform or repent or you are out of our guild, or you will never get in it. And I wonder whether any profession is immune from that kind of problem.

I have heard law students ask questions about the law—ask who has access to lawyers and who doesn't and who gets sentenced to what length of prison term and who gets pardoned and who doesn't. But I have also heard them say that there is just so far one can go as a student or young lawyer with questions like those. Suppose a young architect starts asking about the purposes to which his profession often lends itself. Suppose he asks why millions of people live in shacks, and get nothing built for them, while others spend millions of dollars on a building meant to indulge the "tastes" of a particular man and his wife. I can imagine a teacher of architecture asking the young architect: What is your *problem?* Don't you *want* to be an architect? Do you have something *troubling* you about our profession?

Berrigan: It seems to me that the hopeful thing about everything we've been discussing is that the best of the young people are no longer taking it on the chin, bending and scraping before that kind of "ten commandments from on high."

Coles: Are you sure?

Berrigan: Haven't you seen a new attitude among medical students recently?

Coles: Yes. But perhaps I tend to be pessimistic. I worry that the kind of spirit we have seen in the finest of medical students and law students and divinity students in recent years will gradually be subdued—because in the South in the early sixties I saw many young idealists get discouraged and give up. You keep talking about the war; well, we will settle this war, and then I doubt so many of our young will be as aroused as they recently have been. I am not at all sure that this nation is changing as much as some social critics say it is; nor do I believe the majority of our people want any really drastic changes in the way the nation is set up.

Berrigan: You mention that the war will eventually end. One can only hope and pray for that day. But I don't think the war is the only thing that upsets our young people. For many youths, the war and the way we have fought it and our reasons for fighting it—all of that is symptomatic of something much deeper. I am not hopeful about what I see happening simply because the war has prompted young people to rebel against this or that. It seems to me that many youths I have met in seminaries, in law schools, in graduate schools, have their sights on a very large picture indeed; they are drawing analogies and making connections between evil abroad and evil at home, exploitation in South America or Southeast Asia and exploitation in the business world and in the professions and universities. The professional horror that they are subjected to by explicit and implicit pressures no longer paralyzes certain students; rather, they are as outraged by lies and deceit in a teacher or doctor or local politician as they are by the spectacle of this nation's international behavior, its coziness with Latin American dictators and Greek dictators and the Spanish one and feudal oil barons in the Middle East. In the university, the essential character of the society comes across; no matter what students are told to read, the values of the world outside those college gates constantly intrude. That is to say, the university's connections, its sources of power and money, and the way the university responds to the pressures exerted on it by those various sources—all of that is a microcosm of the country at large. If students get to see the connection, get to see how politicians and military leaders and industrialists and yes, I am sorry to say, our religious leaders all work together, get to see how professors join in the act, too, and help make poison gas or pesticides that hurt children, help run that "military-industrial complex" Dwight Eisenhower spoke of—well, if students get to see all of that, they've had some important boot-camp training; I mean they have learned how our society works, and they're in a better position to fight for *their* beliefs, rather than surrender and take orders from above. They are less naïve. They know we aren't *suddenly* asked to serve the beast; all the way along, from our first years in school, we learn to do so.

So, I can see how you would feel gloomy, but there are good reasons to feel otherwise. I have talked to students in a number of campuses and am impressed with their determination, come what may, to get at the heart of things, look at the bared bones of our society, at the junctures of power in it, analyze the relationship of the trustees of universities to those who run our corporations and own mines or plantations in the Third World. And I don't see those students getting gloomy. Perhaps they never intend to make the compromises you and I may have felt were necessary to become a Jesuit or a psychiatrist—to become "acceptable" and "accredited" professional men!

Coles: Perhaps you are right—or perhaps you romanticize those youths. They can no doubt be blind and mean, like other human beings. They can no doubt trick themselves, as well as others. I believe anyone's mind can fool itself, can draw veils over certain "areas" or "subjects," can resort to illusions, can protect itself from what you call the "bare bones" of reality. Even people who say that their life work is dedicated to finding out what reality is, be it psychological reality, or the social reality a novelist's sensibility often tries to evoke, or the reality of "physical matter" a scientist studies—even those people know how to whistle in the dark and spin elaborate fantasies (sometimes called "theories") and ignore all kinds of things, while emphasizing what it suits their purposes to emphasize as citizens of a particular nation and as men or women alive at a certain moment in history. By design, witting or unwitting, we blind ourselves at certain moments. We are actively clever at not seeing a lot. Our language and literature is riddled with available masks and disguises. In a sense we are all like Blanche Dubois—whom we can laugh at and think of as a pathetic New Orleans woman, a character out of a strange Southern Gothic mind. Yet how much like her some of us are—able to make our accommodations, to camouflage ourselves and our beliefs, and to see only what we can safely see.

Berrigan: But how much *can* one safely see?

Coles: I think it is an individual matter, to some extent—and of course different nations allow their citizens different degrees of leeway. But one has always to ask: what is it that people don't want to see about the world around them, and why?

Berrigan: I'd like to suggest that the power of seeing grows in the very act of seeing. And that the innate health of the eye grows in the very exercise of the eye. I've encountered so much hopelessness—even among young people; and I am referring to the hopelessness of people who see their fellow human beings as incorrigible, as beyond change. Perhaps they don't dare *look*—see the more positive things, the more encouraging signs. We can trick ourselves into despair as well as false optimism! Many of the most sensitive young feel themselves constantly assaulted; and they see no likelihood that those in power, either in the university or in the government or in public life or professional life are going to become anything other than they are. And, of course, once that view of things becomes a general interpretation of life, then the worst sort of despair follows. Perhaps those who despair resort to their own kind of illusions—and one sees fine young people do so.

Coles: I'd like to tell you something and ask you to respond. Six years ago Stokely Carmichael and I together gave a seminar on nonviolence to the college students who went South to Mississippi for the so-called Mississippi Summer Project. Now in that six year period of time I think it is publicly known how Stokely has changed his ideas—in what direction. Meanwhile I continue to do my work, and I say to myself: I haven't become bitter the way he is; I haven't left the country the way he has done; I haven't said some of the things that he has said, about violence being as American as apple pie; I haven't felt myself wanting to denounce my country as vigorously and sweepingly as he has. And so I say I am somehow not *bitter*, not *depressed*, not in a *rage*. I tell myself I haven't gone down the road of anger and despair and unqualified or irrational political estrangement. And, of course, I say to myself that I haven't done all that, gone in that direction, because I'm a white middle class doctor, and I haven't been waging the struggle that Stokely Carmichael has. Yet I wonder whether it cannot be said that in the last five years he has in fact grown and become increasingly aware and sensitive to various issues—and it is for *that* reason he has moved away from the joint position he and I held in 1964, the joint political and social analysis we made for the "students" we "taught" before they went South to Jackson and the Delta.

I suppose it can be argued that what I fancy to be my "maturity" and "equanimity" and "good sense" and "historical distance" are really all signs of my death. In other words, because of the life I lead I am every day protected and sheltered from the concrete realities that affect (every minute of every day) ninety percent of the people on this planet. It can also be argued that I am fatally compromised, and that my way of looking both at Stokely's political position and his psychological development, as well as at the economic and social realities of the world around me, reflects my willingness to live as I do, indeed my desire to live as I do, which the critic of people like me would say means living as the beneficiary of a colonial world power, able to command resources from wretchedly poor lands and turn them into the style of living a man like me enjoys, while even in his own land, let alone Africa or South America or Asia, millions live half-desperate lives. In other words the way I look at Stokely and his development in the last five or six years (as evidence of deterioration, stress, disintegration, violence) is a measure of my own predicament. Do you follow what I am trying to say?—that when I talk about him as I do I am really describing my own situation, my own cast of mind, and mode of existence. The way I look at him and his behavior is really a way of expressing my own relationship to a particular society.

Berrigan: Well, I'm glad such thoughts are at least occurring to you! It's important for people like us to feel uneasy, to turn on ourselves with questions. I don't want to be self-congratulatory when I say that. I just think we have to look at ourselves as others see us—for reasons we too easily can forget. I don't have access to Stokely Carmichael, I haven't known him, so I can't add much to your remarks. I would be inclined to go a little bit easier on some of the language he has used these recent years. I don't consider him as bitter and angry as you do. I tried to tell you earlier that the blacks I knew at Cornell were struggling, among other things, with the problem of language. Their fiery, heated-up ghetto language, in my own experience, was a way of insisting upon being heard, understood and heard —by people they feared were deaf, dumb, and blind. I find in many cases a profound dichotomy between the way blacks conducted their lives and the way they spoke about their lives; they shout to Whitey but they live among and for themselves. Many of the so-called "militant" and "extremist" blacks I knew at Cornell showed themselves capable of leading quite peaceable and quite humane lives among themselves; but they presented a different face to us, as they said, out of the need to survive. They considered us to be bestial, and in many cases they were right—witness the cowardly burning down of their black studies program by a gang last Easter.

Coles: It may be bestial for an observer like me to characterize people (whether they be men like Stokely Carmichael or the students at Cornell) with words like *violent, frustrated, embittered,* while at the same time failing to mention the bitterness and violence and frustration and moodiness and despair his own world generates among its supporters, never mind its critics. Given a certain historical context the acts of those six young students at Cornell or Stokely's development in the last six years don't seem so strange or so clinically psychopathological. Certainly historians like Richard Hofstadter have shown us how deep and wide are the currents of violence in America.

Berrigan: I would want to hear what a black psychiatrist would say. Would he find Stokely Carmichael or the Cornell students exceptional? If so, I would have to stop and think; but I doubt he would.

Cole: Do you think his black skin would protect him from the white professional values that we've been talking about?

Berrigan: Well, that's a good question. I can't answer it.

Coles: Has black skin protected seminarians from the pitfalls of their profession?

Berrigan: Perhaps, in some cases. I'm not sure. I wouldn't want to excuse a black seminarian of one thing or another he did or didn't do, simply because he was black. But I *would* want to be careful, very careful before I came out with those "liberal," evenhanded judgments that whites often use as a means of ignoring the special history, the special circumstances of life with which black people have to contend. With respect to a black seminarian, before I said anything to "judge" him, I would want to know how he conducts himself with his people. I would want to know whether he has been able to build a compassionate and loving community where he works. I suspect many black priests have been able to do so. I think people like us ought to stand outside and distinguish at all times between the way a black man acts with Whitey, and the way he acts in his own world. Those are two very different things.

Coles: Yes, and it's a distinction we don't often draw. I mean, there is the black man as the white man's devil, and the black man as he is in his own world, to which the white man has no access. Nevertheless, I wonder how redemptive one's skin color can actually be. I doubt that skin color will save blacks from the kinds of tensions we've been talking about—the bitterness, the meanness man is heir to. Certainly I've seen bitterness and meanness and vicious kinds of exploitation in the black communities—and I don't think I now speak as a white observer. I mean, I've seen physical evidence of it: black people hurting black people, black people cheating black people, robbing them, assaulting them. Nor is that a very unique experience on my part. Blacks have written about such matters—yes, I would say written about the *humanity* of their people. I kept on wondering as you were talking about North Vietnam, whether the kinds of violence and horror that we've just been talking about don't in some way exist there. After all, they have shown themselves capable of hunting down people, killing them. I don't believe the North Vietnamese people—and certainly not its government—are beyond the sins our people, our government demonstrate.

Berrigan: Yes, we should go into all of that, and those are important issues. Perhaps we can distinguish people by what they emphasize about "human nature." It seems to me that I search out in any given situation whatever elements of hope I can find there—I hope not by way of self-deception. Yes, one has to acknowledge the horror of life, the violence and the bloodletting and all the rest of it, be it found among blacks or whites or North Vietnamese or South Vietnamese. But we have to keep looking for signs of a future: those signs that we try to discern and even to follow, perhaps to enlarge, to give breathing space to. One must keep those signs at the eye's center, because I think they are the object of one's true search. What is best in man? What is most hopeful in man? What can be built upon in any particular situation? The other side of the picture is obviously there, but it belongs in the eye's peripheral vision. I just don't believe that the truth of things is revealed to us by our cynical, hoarding, businesslike, materialist political philosophers who see evil everywhere—as a means of justifying their own evil. Truth was revealed to us by Jesus Christ, and those who in lesser ways follow His tradition.

Coles: Christ was killed.

Berrigan: Yes, yes—but His truth didn't die; the truth of His life and of other lives remains available to us.

Coles: Jesus Christ had a moment of extreme doubt before He died, felt that He had been betrayed, asked why He was forsaken. Isn't that also a part of the reality of man? In all lives doubt and a sense of abandonment are there, and may well be dominant, at least in a given life. Again, Christ died sad, and afraid all His effort was for naught.

Berrigan: Yes, I would agree.

Coles: You are saying, though, that each man has to choose which of the themes in Christ's life will obsess him, so to speak; and the choice determines the character of the man's life. The way one looks at the world, what one does in one's life, has to do with whether one emphasizes the negatives or seeks out the positives; and it may well be that it is to a particular society's advantage that we all emphasize the gloomier side of things, because if we do, we needn't trouble ourselves to undertake any great social and political struggles, since they are doomed almost by definition.

Berrigan: You know, it is interesting: as I look back over the last five years, my thinking has moved along two directions, and let me for a second state them, rather than editorialize on them. For one thing I have felt that somehow, however awkwardly and inadequately, I had to keep moving along; that is, I couldn't stop and become satisfied with myself and my various ideas. Rather I had to keep questioning myself, keep taking one step, then another, even though at the time the step seemed difficult and maybe controversial. And then I have felt that I am not alone, that a number of us are together, struggling for certain things, and that we had to stay together, work together.

Cole: "We" being?

Berrigan: Well, "we" are people I know, my brother and those I have loved and worked with; and "we" are thousands and thousands of people I have never known and never will know; and "we" are some fine people I have met these past weeks while underground. I have learned how much I need others, how much we need one another in this world. You no doubt are aware of the old philosophical struggle between the Manichaean and Christian view of evil. I guess I have tried hard to believe that there is just so much territory that belongs to evil—that one is obliged to refuse evil substantial control over one's life. One must refuse evil so much power that it becomes a shadow over you or an in-dwelling devil. At one time I know I was in trouble. I not only feared the Pentagon, for example: I *believed* in it—I believed its power was *there,* and "there" in a way that transcends mere "fact." I mean, I despaired. I felt it was hopeless to fight such a monstrous thing. But somehow I survived that kind of thinking. I learned "hope," perhaps. I learned to have confidence in others and myself—in the power that one's faith and love can exert—yes, even on the Pentagon.

Coles: But you don't think your viewpoint is idiosyncratic, a function of particular psychological qualities in you; you see that hope in others and you see *conversions* possible—you see a point to fighting against the tendency we all have to despair.

Berrigan: I would say that by the grace of God I am able to draw upon something quite important and healthy in a long tradition, and I find around me constantly manifestations of that "something" in the lives of other people—no matter what tradition and what background *they* happen to draw upon for spiritual strength. For all the bad and evil to be found on this planet, I find much goodness struggling for birth and struggling for expression. So I do not feel alone; I do not feel lonely or eccentric. I feel the kind of steadfastness one experiences in the presence of others—and I am sure we together will persist and keep struggling for what we believe important as long as we are permitted to live.

Coles: Do you possess the strength to work with—and by you I mean more than you as an individual—the problems of millions and millions of plain, ordinary middle class Americans who don't have the same concerns and aspirations you have, or at least don't demonstrate those concerns in a way that seems to be politically active and responsive to the injustices of the world? Or are you and others you feel close to confining yourselves to those who for various reasons welcome you as allies —certain youths, certain blacks, certain poor people? I'm asking about whether there is to be a ministry to suburbia, a ministry to the professions, a ministry to the American workingman —not necessarily made up only of ministers, but an effort to find in people who seem without your particular concerns a larger measure of compassion and selflessness and integrity than some of our social critics are willing to allow, or even think to wonder about.

Berrigan: Well, I hope I don't sound hardhearted when I say that one does what one is called upon to do, and lives in a certain way and perhaps dies in a certain way. We do what we can, and none of us does it very well. Sometimes the majority of a nation proves itself wise beyond words; sometimes that majority becomes fatally blind. I feel responsible for a very small area of life. I can only do what I can do.

Coles: You feel you have enough to do clarifying the ethical dimensions of your own life, and of the relative handful of lives you affect.

Berrigan: I hope I am governed by Camus's sense of modesty. In his treatment of his heroes and his treatment also of political questions, Camus reveals a very deep sense of himself as a modest being in the world. That is to say, he was a man who refused to enter into questions which are of quantity, so to speak. He didn't judge himself by the number of bodies he reached, by the "converts" he made, by the "power" he amassed or the "influence" he was credited with having. Indeed when he *was* called influential or successful or whatever, he worried a great deal, because he knew how corrupting a certain kind of "fame" can be. He had a certain length of time to live (we never do know how much, do we?) and he had a certain measure of talent—and he assumed that if he spent his time wisely and worked hard, then *something* would occur. And by the same token, something occurs because you write, something occurs because I write, something occurs because you are who you are and have been where you have been, and the same for me. A lot of what we achieve we don't even know about; sometimes inklings of it come through to us—in letters we get, in responses of students and people, in all that goes on in the world as a result of what we say or write or do. Now those responses are important; they are important not only to my ego, but as a corrective. Through others one learns what is happening, how one's ideas are in keeping with the world—and we can never know the world if we stay apart, rely upon ourselves too exclusively. And yet I have to qualify what I just said, because I really do believe that when one is at his deepest with himself, the outside world—here I refer to the so-called "pressures" of conformity—means relatively little. For instance when I went to Catonsville or when I went to Hanoi or when I went on trial or when I went underground, I didn't have around me voices that urged me on, or wide support which enabled me to feel I was doing an approved and thoroughly respectable thing. I would mistrust that kind of approval very much.

Coles: You mean you have never asked the Gallup Poll (or commissioned a private pollster to find out) how the American public "feels" about your ideas or actions.

Berrigan: No; it would have been unnecessary. I knew at those various critical times in my life what many of my countrymen felt. I don't mean to say that at those points I was without friends and considerable support from people I have never met, and probably will never meet. But my friends are themselves often struggling against considerable odds; what they offered me was a certain light that emanated from their lives. In one way or another they said to me: you are somewhere and we are somewhere and you come and tell us what you have finally decided, and we will stand with you as best we can.

Coles: What you just said sounds like what you're now doing: you hope to reach out toward people, hope to bring them (I guess in an evangelical way) nearer to where you're at. You want people to take steps, strides even, because they have heard you, felt your message, responded. You want us to be different doctors, different teachers—and different citizens.

Berrigan: Yes, but I wouldn't put it that way, because I have a distrust of leading people—and especially I don't think people have to be exactly where others are whom they happen to meet and like. I would rather help those I talk with get a deeper understanding of where they are and let our lives and aims gradually converge—here the word has to be a little vague. I get uneasy when it is suggested that I have come upon some final solution—a horrible phrase used by another gentleman to describe the destruction of millions of people. What we are really searching for are the many valuable things that must be done if a very complex society like ours is to be reborn again—made humane, rendered less paralyzed by its obsessions and fears and conceits. It's a very large order. I believe it's a thousand year project; I don't think this thing is going to be finished in my lifetime or in anybody's lifetime. I think we possibly can get something new started that will open doors, start currents, generate energies. When I was reminded by the Vietnamese that their revolution is really a thousand years old, that they have been an occupied people for the longest stretches of that history, that they are only the most recent heirs to a struggle, I felt that they were saying something important.

Coles: They have a sense of history that I guess some of us don't have.

Berrigan: Well, they have a sense of patience with history that I know I don't have—patience not as coolie victims or nigger victims, but the kind of patience which thoughtful people call upon as they pursue a slow, difficult, but utterly necessary task.

Coles: It is certainly a historical irony that those people and us are now antagonists. There is such an obvious contrast between our view of the present, of the immediate, of what has to be done in *this* life, and the Vietnamese sense of history and time as reassuring companions—not to be defied or challenged or "overcome," but lived with and even smiled at. No wonder men like Ho Chi Minh have confused (perhaps bedeviled is the word) Americans—who simply cannot comprehend such a view of what life is. Some people think of their nation's history as almost infinitely ongoing: centuries have preceded them, and centuries will follow them. Because of America's youth, and its sudden emergence as a nation of people who came from other nations—well, clearly we have a sense of *time* that differs markedly from the sense of time the Vietnamese or the Chinese have, even as the Russians have a sense about *space* that one invader after another has learned about only too late.

Berrigan: It is interesting, too, that there have been mysterious meeting points between the North Vietnamese and us, between their sensibilities and ours—based upon their perhaps naïve reading of our revolution. Bernard Fall tells in his book that in the early fifties when Ho Chi Minh finally began the task of setting down a blueprint for his nation, a document that would be equivalent to our Declaration of Independence, he searched all over for a text of the American Constitution and the Declaration of Independence. He was determined to incorporate into the Vietnamese "declaration" certain phrases out of our own "declaration" that he had come across when he had been in the United States. Finally a copy of our Declaration of Independence was flown in, and he sat down and used it extensively—which is apparent to anyone who goes over the first draft, available to the observer in Hanoi. And today, as you and I talk about such things, we have to remind ourselves that July the fourth, an important national holiday of ours, has just passed by. As I reflect on this country I don't want to be pessimistic. Maybe Ho Chi Minh had good reason to call upon our Declaration of Independence. Maybe this country is capable of moving in directions that will surprise and edify the world.

Coles: You are now more hopeful about America than you seem to think others in other countries have any reason to be.

Berrigan: Revolutionary fervor is a mysterious substance and a mysterious resource, too. A man like Ho Chi Minh can sometimes be more hopeful about his enemy than the enemy is about themselves. By the same token, I feel those of us here who are fighting to make the country more peaceful ought not to give up on our own people—give up on the possibilities in human beings, however fearful they have grown up to be.

Coles: Maybe those struggling against great odds, like the North Vietnamese, have to bear themselves that way—or risk bitterness, which is all too soon followed by despair.

Berrigan: Yes, I think so. Visitors to Hanoi would leave with the feeling that there is such idealism at work in their regard for us that it would almost stretch us to respond in kind as best we can. Maybe that's the way love operates, in that commonly we grow within friendship or within marriage because of the purity and the idealism of other people in our regard. I think I have found that in my own family.

Coles: Returning once more to the question of professional life. What might professional men do—in the tradition of your deeds? Or is it impossible to prescribe for others? I mean, you have taken a step as a clergyman in relationship to the law, the federal law. You did something, were judged, were sentenced, and have now taken a position in what you call the underground. Could you let your mind wander for others?

Berrigan: Could I again point to some examples? I have in mind a lawyer who was heavily involved in the Chicago trial; he was also on our legal staff, and he seemed deeply moved by his exposure to us. He went out to the Milwaukee trial after our trial and he defended those people out there, and then he went on to Chicago. But I don't want to talk about his public record, but rather what occurred as he talked to me during the time of our trial. I guess I was perhaps his closest friend in our Catonsville group, and the one most available timewise. He wanted to talk to me not only about what it meant for me to do what I did at Catonsville, but about broader issues, like the purposes of the worker priests in France. He asked about them, and I said yes, I was over there and knew many of them, knew them at their hour of greatest trouble in 1954, when they were facing suppression by Pius XII. The lawyer said he'd done a certain amount of reading on the worker priests and I suggested further reading and he did the reading. He was intrigued with the professional implications of the struggle waged by the worker priests; he wanted to apply their example to himself and the legal profession in general. Certain clerics had moved to the edge of the clerical estate and had joined a very different cultural and political and religious scene, and were finding out what it was to be a priest under very tough conditions. Perhaps, he thought, lawyers should do likewise.

When I met him a few months after the trial he said: I want to show you the text I have of a talk I did at Harvard, at the law school. In the text he drew upon the analogy of the worker priests over and over again. What he was moving toward in his own life was what later became the "lawyers' caucus" in New York. He moved out of his lawyer's office on the East Side and went over to a loft on the West Side—in a very different neighborhood, in the company of a few other young lawyers. They set up an office which will be increasingly available to poor people or people waging a struggle against America's military and political foreign policy. Now, that lawyer had decided he could not remain at the center of his profession—and embark upon occasional expeditions into extracurricular political activities. He had decided that his whole life must move over. I found that decision very sound; I found it very much like what happened to me.

Coles: Such a decision, or move, if made by professional men, would confront them directly with their society and with the courts and with police and also confront their families—to come back to the families again. How are middle class children going to fare when and if their parents take political stands which involve the risk of prison and the sacrifice not only of career but even of enough money to get by? For that matter, how do the individual professional men themselves fare? You would probably say that they don't do it as individuals. I note you brought up an example of a *group* of lawyers. I suppose those lawyers had to come together not only as professional men; I mean, their families have to come together in some way, too.

Berrigan: Right. And I think lawyers need help in such a struggle from others, from doctors or teachers, from workers of all kinds.

Coles: Do you see any real developments along such lines right now?

Berrigan: If you or someone had asked me even five years ago what group of people is most intransigent and hopeless, so far as all this is concerned, I would immediately have answered clerics, clerics obviously. And I would have answered with despair. But then all of a sudden something happened, and clerics were at Catonsville and clerics were at Milwaukee and clerics were in

Chicago, clerics were all over the place—not in great numbers, true, but they were there, and that to me evokes hope. I wonder what I would say today if someone asked me to name the most intransigent, hopeless group of people.

Coles: Perhaps you would say psychiatrists?

Berrigan: No, I would say that the problem now is not a particular profession, but the family—indeed the whole society.

6 • Inside and Outside the Church

Coles: I'd like to ask you how unique you consider your experience as a fugitive priest? We are now being told on radio and television and in newspapers and magazines that this is the first time that a Catholic priest has been a fugitive from justice. As I read and listen to those accounts I find myself thinking of our past, our history. What do we in fact know about our history? Who teaches us the history we learn? What don't we ever find out about our past? A teacher of mine when I was in fifth grade used to say, "history, twistory," and I've never forgotten that— because it's quite clear that what we learn about our past is determined by those who have their own reasons to notice this, ignore that, write about one thing and omit mention of something else. We are only now beginning to realize how distorted our history books have been so far as blacks and Indians are concerned. The issue often is one of blatant misrepresentation by historians; but more subtly, a certain tone or shade of emphasis can also lead the reader far along into an ideological position which he confuses with a statement of "fact." So, I wonder about the history of the underground in America and other countries. I wonder how unique and surprising and unprecedented your behavior is. I have the impression that this country was founded by people from England who had been in the underground. Not only were many of our first settlers in the underground in England, but in addition they fled, they became exiles; so it was exiles and ex-members of a religious underground who started the United States of America. And then one wonders, apart from the underground railroad in the nineteenth century, whether there isn't a tradition in this country of dissent similar to yours, a tradition whereby people not only say controversial things, but take action that challenges the society in a more significant way, a more comprehensive or unnerving way—and do so without immediately surrendering themselves to sheriffs and judges. I am thinking of the South and Appalachia and the Southwest, where the needs of "justice" as well as "banditry" have prompted men to defy authorities believed to be corrupt, or worse.

Berrigan: I do believe very much that what I am doing has a tradition behind it. As for what you now hear about me, I believe in this country one constantly has to contend with the ahistorical and sensational aspects of our news media. We see every day how a "folklore" of sorts is created, how the words and acts of particular individuals are written about and talked about wildly, uncritically, hysterically, romantically, foolishly. And certainly in our culture, religion and the words or deeds of religious men are just more grist for the mills that the media run. I mean, every breakaway from the so-called "norm" is going to be a headline for the media, who obviously are interested in all kinds of *grotesquerie* and deviation. I really don't know whether it's useful any longer to consider my status or that of my brother in the light of the Roman Catholic segment of the population. It seems to me that it's much more useful to consider what I am doing in relation to a broad spectrum of dissent that goes back, as you just said, to the act of leaving Europe and settling here, then waging a revolution against England, a colonial power.

While we were in jail in Catonsville I learned about the career of an eighteenth-century American priest whose real name is not even known; evidently he used the alias, John Urey. Very little is known about him except by hearsay and by reports and comments written about him after his death. He was executed and his execution was not recorded; his trial was blacked out, and the very disposition of his body was never revealed. But during those years before the American Revolution, when we were well into our terrible and brutal treatment of blacks, this man (who as far as I can piece it together was an émigré from Ireland) landed in Manhattan and shortly thereafter launched himself on a career of harboring fugitive slaves from the West Indies, and getting them North through Manhattan. He is said to have settled in the back room of an Irish pub in the lower East Side of Manhattan, and operated by night out of there. When runaway slaves were caught they were drawn and quartered, burned and lynched. And eventually he, too—after some six years of "illegal activity"—shared the fate of the slaves; he was swiftly killed. So there was an inspiring, mysterious figure out of our national mists for us to think about when we were in jail. At our sentencing I had composed a poem in his honor and read it that day; I hoped to link our fate with his, even though we had not been tested as he was, or shown his degree of lonely courage —and yes, willingness to defy the established "law and order" and the "tradition" of his day.

But in general, alas, one can't make very great claims about the heroism of religious figures in American history. I think especially the Catholic Church has been very late in catching up with anything that remotely might be called its own tradition. Catholics in large numbers came to this country relatively late and came as large "ethnic" groups, each impoverished and frightened and essentially oriented toward winning its own place in the sun; for these reasons I think social and political radicalism could not take root. Up until very recently, say five or ten years ago, not only the hierarchy but the overwhelming majority of the Church's intellectual and theological leaders were intensely loyal to America's foreign policy. I think in this regard the death of Cardinal Spellman was particularly significant. For a quarter of a century Spellman stood loyally, arm in arm, with the John Foster Dulleses of this nation. Spellman's international prestige, his connection with figures like Churchill and Pius XII and Roosevelt—all of that militated against anything very powerful rising from beneath. And of course I had a firsthand taste of his ideas and his power. He exiled me from New York and from the country.

Coles: You had a personal encounter with him?

Berrigan: It was personal in the sense that he found even so unexciting an organization as Clergy and Laymen Concerned About Vietnam a very personal affront. He and his subalterns were outraged. It was simply intolerable that a priest in his own diocese would make a beginning like this with Jews and Protestants. So I was very quickly got rid of. On the other hand, one can point to the fact that there has been, at least since the twenties, through the Catholic Worker Movement especially, a very solid tradition of biblical dissent from war; and one can also reflect that the first symbolic draft card burnings were centered in the Catholic community, and that as protest advanced into assaults upon draft boards it was in the beginning also a Catholic enterprise. So, I guess one might remember, as Francine Gray has noted, that out of the worst something very new and inspiring can emerge, such is the irony of history. Of course our Protestant communities have never been under the type of suppression that Catholics have on these social issues; whereas we Catholics have been subjected to the iron hand of authority. Again and again we have heard the Church speak—on an astonishing range of subjects; and we have been told that once the Church has spoken, one must bow one's head and say yes, yes, yes. As an American Catholic, an American priest, you could always point to the fine and progressive statements that have come out of Rome on social issues; but the Church here for decades and decades never really responded to those papal encyclicals.

I guess that's a long way of saying a very simple thing: more and more Catholics, a distinct minority but still a significant minority, are finally able to see their place in the tradition of Christianity, and able to gain a much wider and more enlightened perspective on their place, and able to go ahead and work at what *they* believe right (rather than obey blindly the Spellmans of this land) and do that work with their brothers from other faiths. So in the last five years of this war we Catholics have been able to offer a certain leavening, a certain direction, to the peace movement. Not that Protestants and Jews haven't also had their moral and ethical struggles. Even recently one would hear in only half jest that churches like the Episcopal Church could be depended upon to lend us their real estate for actions like Catonsville, but they were often unwilling to *participate* in an effort like Catonsville. In any event, in spite of the tremendous hold on Catholics that the Church has, and in spite of the tight discipline of the priesthood and of religious orders, something was evidently gathering, some waters of human passion and concern were rising—were reaching a boiling point— and then, suddenly (it seems to me concurrently with Pope John's whole breakthrough) the kettle tipped over, the brew spilled, and—well, things will never be exactly the same again.

But, to answer your question a little bit more exactly: it seems to me that Roman Catholic identity as such is unimportant, given the times and the real issues. My brother and I have no continuing interest whatsoever in what you might call the internal questions of the Catholic community, whether that be the question of parochial schools or the question of birth control or the question of celibacy; we look upon such matters as in essence retarded questions of a community that still has to catch up with Christ's invitation that all men come join Him, and be with Him—in all their variety. And how sad it is that in the face of the terrible, terrible issues which face this planet's two billion human beings, some in the Church, priests and bishops as well as laymen, continue to be so utterly self-centered, so narrow, so uninterested in others, so aggrandizing—in the name of Jesus Christ! So let the Church "catch up" through the efforts of others; and I say that not to be arrogant, but to emphasize how urgent are the tasks that all too few of us are taking the trouble to attend. My brother Phil and I are interested in a kind of raw fundamentalism that has to do with the stance of the Church before mankind; we want to help the Church make that stance, we want to do what we can in *that* direction. We will join with other communities, Catholic or non-Catholic, religious or thoroughly secular—so long as their seriousness and passion are manifest.

Coles: But you are loyal to the Church, which is, after all, an institution.

Berrigan: I hope so.

Coles: I suppose I should say that you are loyal to what you conceive to be the spirit of the Church, or loyal to what you would want the Church to be. You are not ready to stop being a Catholic.

Berrigan: By no means. In fact, I think I shared with you when we were not taping our conversations my sense of shock at seeing the statement by David Miller in which he asserts that he no longer considers himself a Catholic. I hope with all my heart that he still considers himself a Christian. I cannot but consider it a great loss when any person decides that his bonds are broken with the tradition of Christianity.

Coles: Or maybe even with his own past.

Berrigan: Yes, I'm quite sure that the issue is personal as well as religious or philosophical. I know David and I know what he experienced in jail. Most difficult for a man like David, ironically, are the church services one meets up with in prison. He has very deep reasons for being embittered. The chaplains who work in prisons and the army can sometimes be totally militarized men, totally lost in their service to Caesar. They have nothing to offer such young idealistic people; indeed their presence among those youths is a horror and a tragedy for the men and women concerned. It's no wonder that when they are released from jail they walk away in disgust from their own past, from the Church. My hope is that their essential goodness and their connection with the truth of history and of their times will help to lead them (perhaps through a deep and painful path) back to something—and if not specifically to the Catholic community, then to some other community of faith. But we'll have to wait and see on all of that.

Coles: Yet you also say you have no interest in many of the pressing doctrinal and polemical issues that the Church itself is preoccupied with—birth control, celibacy, the institutional matters of the Church.

Berrigan: Well, we're now getting back to something we spoke of earlier. Who decides which questions are important—and for whom? Because a Cardinal Spellman happens to think something is important and urgent does not mean I have to agree—and put my energies into his concerns. My brother and I feel that there's been a tremendous dislocation of true consciousness for a long time in the American Catholic community. Perhaps in the past, because so many Catholics were the immigrant underdogs of the nineteenth century, the Church had to be narrowly preoccupied with its own power, even as its parishioners were. But in the late twentieth century the Catholic community is thoroughly a part of the American social and economic and political scene—hence we have a corresponding obligation to look outward, extend ourselves, reach across national and racial and ideological barriers. My brother and I feel that there's an important chapter of history to be written in our own time, and we would like to help write it. It is a chapter of history which, we hope, will see the center of the Church's concerns located at the edge of society—where human lives are involved in a really tragic struggle for survival and human dignity. Phil and I believe it is even selfish for us to get involved with that struggle—because out of it we will all, perhaps, get a new and vital sense of what it is to be a Christian. What is most precious to us are the elements in our faith that sustain us, and those elements are very mysterious and very difficult to speak about. I often feel that to be asked what is essential to you in your faith is almost as delicate and secret a matter as to be asked what are the elements of a good marriage. And by the same token I am often appalled by the superficiality and the vulgarity of mind that is revealed in those discussions of "what Jesus means" and "what the church means"—and on and on.

Coles: There are similar all too pietistic discussions of "marriage"—many of them these days dismally laced with psychological and psychiatric terms.

Berrigan: Some things are so close to the heart's core that they are reflected in the quality of one's life, and defy verbalization. But the analogy is very meaningful to me: faith is like marriage; faith has its fits and starts, its fevers and chills. To borrow from Robert Frost, a Catholic man of faith inevitably will have a lover's quarrel with the Church. The believer feels quarrelsome as well as devout and obedient. What is most important to Phil and me, I believe, is the historical truth manifested in the actuality of Jesus, and the community which we believe is in continuity with His spirit and His presence—a presence which makes certain rigorous and specific demands on man at any period of time. One's life style inevitably prompts a debate of sorts with the Church, even as we both comply with, and wage our struggles with, the powers-that-be of the society to which we belong. Right now, interestingly enough, I find myself less and less in trouble with the Church, and more and more in trouble with the state. I mean, the Jesuits are more and more thoughtful about the issues that Phil and I and others have tried to raise. Even though there is no massive support within the order there is a definite unease—perhaps of the kind that precedes and accompanies awakening on the part of many people. By the way, Philip doesn't have as strong or passionate a sense of belonging to his order as I do with regard to mine. I think I know why. I think it's fair to say that his congregation's traditions are by no means as old or as exciting or as imaginative; his order hasn't undergone the test of so many cultures for so long a period, and there hasn't been by any means within that order an understanding of what he was trying to do—either in civil rights or in the peace movement. I feel I have at least been understood; maybe not rallied around, given explicit sanction, but understood, yes.

Coles: How would you characterize Phil's work in the South? Didn't the Josephite brothers have a certain tradition for that kind of work?

Berrigan: Well, I think for him that kind of work is finished. And in the light of what has happened in this country recently, we ought to reexamine just what the Josephite brothers were doing when they went South to teach black children. Often they were used to help local priests and bishops evade their own responsibilities—to help them dismiss blacks as outside their area of concern. No wonder the order is now going through intense self-scrutiny about such practices. The idea of a white priestly ministry to black people is of course growing more and more unworkable. Phil really doesn't have much news any more from the order, because progressively they have sort of cut themselves off from him; but among the younger men he says there is a sense that the whole chapter of the last sixty or seventy years has been closed, and the question of where they go from here remains open and by no means easily settled. But where *isn't* it difficult for priests these days? I think that the Jesuits, in a more complex way, are involved in an analogous kind of stalemate; they are still scrambling up their various academic slopes, still trying to plant their flags at the top—while at the very same time many of those who have reached the top are yelling back that it's useless up there, it's barren up there. I have noticed that often the Jesuit graduate students studying in the Ivy League colleges quickly tend either to grow very quickly (in which case they want to do more than study, study,

study) or else they begin to wither away. So one can only hope that the "freedom" that secular colleges offer priests will help them in more than academic ways—though I'm afraid from what I saw at Yale and at Cornell there is no way we can be sure the best rather than the worst will happen.

Coles: Would you spell out the "worst" that you say can happen to such Jesuits?

Berrigan: Yes, I should try to do so. I don't mean to be harsh; I'm trying to be as objective as I can. I am simply saying that some Jesuits at places like Yale and Cornell and Harvard join all too uncritically whatever academic "scene" they happen to have come upon. They can even become caricatures of the Ivy League snob. They seem to have the idea that all they need do is study and earn the approval of their professors and eventually return with honors to Jesuit campuses and to the Jesuit communities. It is as if they need a parchment, a plenary indulgence, if one can speak in old Church terms. Then they can clutch hold of the certificate and be sure they will soon enter the higher echelon of Jesuit operations. And how sad! They are, after all, priests, men of God. I fear many of them don't stop and think that even at the level of practicality, students today no longer are so impressed by the various postures and pretenses of the academy. In any event, the haunting question is: What does a Jesuit do with his life these days? For that matter, what do we all do with our lives today?

Coles: Well, you seem to have found an answer to that question for yourself.

Berrigan: I have an answer, but I can scarcely fool myself with the idea that my answer is going to be acceptable in any large sense. I'm hoping that we'll at least cause others to stop and think about certain issues. For instance, my own provincial— he would be the equivalent of our bishop—wrote me within the month and said that he was indeed aware of the questions I was trying to raise. He is finishing up a job he has held for a number of years and is now looking for opportunities to serve in one of the small Southern colleges. He is going to move away, try to live in a different region, make a fresh start. But beyond that, I think it was quite obvious between the lines of his letter that he was no longer inclined to be an organizational man in the order. Today men like him are trying to find a place where their profession will be useful, and just as important, a place where they can really demonstrate in everyday work the breadth and depth of their ethical concerns. So, they are turning to experimental schooling, North or South, or to social service work— to things like that.

Coles: Then that is the direction the Jesuits and others in the Church are taking—rather than a position of more radical protest, even though I know there are a number of seminarians who pay close attention to your ideas?

Berrigan: I don't really know what to say. These days things happen swiftly and surprisingly. I wonder whether anyone can really know what changes the Catholic Church will undergo in the next few years. I do think that right now priests are leaving all the orders, looking for new ways to serve God; and of course men are leaving the priesthood in great numbers. What they are finding at the other end of things is something I just don't know right now—maybe *they* don't know either. But I am pessimistic—because I don't think a move from the Church to the world really solves the problem. The Church and the secular world are struggling with similar problems, the same problems—so I think quite another kind of move is necessary, one in which the individual challenges more vigorously the assumptions shared by Cardinal Spellman and Richard Nixon, for example.

Coles: Maybe you should go into the reasons for your pessimism in greater detail.

Berrigan: I wonder if instead I could stop for a minute and turn some of the last questions around; they have been very searching questions, the ones you have put to me, and I would like you to respond to them. I would like to know something about your feelings as to what it is to be a Christian in your profession. I would like to know what the Church means to you, what it offers you, and your sense of its future, if any.

Coles: Psychiatry and psychoanalysis today still very much rely upon Freud's view of the mind—at least in America. He was a fearless man, unafraid of a world he had few illusions about. He had a practical and yet brilliantly imaginative mind; he could both observe things with extreme care and then go on to construct theories that are suggestive and illuminating and to this day utterly indispensible for us clinicians. And he was, by self-definition, a conquistador, which means he was ambitious: he wanted to understand more than the particular patients he saw; he wanted to understand the riddles of man's origins and his history. In the course of that quest he wrote a book called *The Future of an Illusion* in which he pretty well indicates what he understood about the nature of religion—in my opinion, a good deal, but not enough. He understood that people delude or comfort themselves, that they often use religious faith to delude or comfort themselves—even as they can use psychiatric and psychoanalytic theories to delude or comfort themselves. He knew very clearly that there is a stale, treacherous, rotten quality to a lot of institutions—among them our churches. I think he was a sharp and canny observer of religious idolatry and blindness, even as in general he had a sharp eye for human blindness and weakness—the frailties of people who don't have the strength to face up to the various kinds of predicaments that we all go through from our early years to the last breath we take. But Freud did not understand, I believe, the genuine, deeply felt religious faith that a person can feel. He seemed to have no comprehension of the order and significance that faith gives to human life. So, I don't really think his ideas about religion are very valuable or important, except for the fact that he justifiably continues to dominate a profession which (such are the ironies of life) has itself become a sort of religion to thousands and thousands of middle class, educated, agnostic Westerners.

I cannot now in a few words tell you all that Christian faith means to me, but I want to mention this: I believe self-centeredness is one of the great temptations and dangers we all have to struggle with—man's apparently inevitable inclination to worship himself, and by extension, his thinking. Nowhere today is this danger greater than in contemporary psychiatry which has become one more secular messianic faith. If you read Freud's writings, or the writings of many other psychoanalysts, you get the sense that if one plumbs the depths of the unconscious, and if one obtains more and more awareness, a new kind of man will emerge. In some of Freud's lectures he expresses the hope that if only larger and larger numbers of people could be psychoanalyzed we would in some way have a better world. Not that psychoanalysis (for some today at the very least an ideology) hasn't made the world significantly different, in the sense that we know more about ourselves. But I constantly find myself suspicious of all man-made ideologies, be they political ones or intellectual ones. To me, going into a church and getting on my knees and praying is something important and almost liberating—but at the same time it is something I don't like to talk about. I was brought up to believe that my faith is no one's business but my own. All I know is that I learned as a child to call upon Isaiah and St. Paul—and I have never wanted to learn to do without either of those two, not to mention Jesus of Nazareth. And I suppose it *is* important for me to state my "dependence" on the biblical writings, because many psychiatrists and psychoanalysts today make such a point of explaining away things, calling things evidence of this or that "problem," and in general taking very little at face value.

Still, it is hard for me to talk about my religious beliefs. I can only say that the people I feel closest to are people like Simone Weil and Georges Bernanos. When I was a resident in psychiatry the person I felt closest to was Paul Tillich. I studied with him. What those "people of grace" have meant to me I cannot put into words. When I have found myself thinking that if only I knew a little more about a person's past or present, if only I knew a little more about his or her mind, then I would be able to "save" him or her, accomplish some psychological miracle, I have usually found myself after a while stopping and instead trying to be much less ambitious—which right then and there can be of help to a patient. At those moments I have been able to ask myself: Save that person for what? Save myself for what? Understand all this for what? In recent times leading psychiatric theorists have insisted that our concepts and even our work must be "value free"—yes, those are the words used. At the same time, of course, we were becoming secular priests to a disenchanted American society. We had some fresh ideas to offer people, but they wanted more, wanted what philosophers and theologians have always offered, some coherent view of an exceedingly hard to fathom world. So we went along and became preachers of sorts. One leading psychoanalytic theoretician used an expression "the average expectable environment"—which was his way of dealing with the so-called "environmental factors" which he saw as a kind of background to the more decisive "internal forces" at work in us. Indeed, for a certain kind of psychoanalyst we grow psychologically as a result of forces at work within the mind which to a great extent are independent of the society in which we live. Now, a man who can talk about "average expectable environment" is a man who has seen a very limited number of patients, all of them quite well-to-do. Ninety percent of the people in this world have no "average expectable environment" but are indeed hungry, even at the edge of starvation, and are living in squalor. One doesn't dismiss the impact of hunger and starvation and severe poverty, with all the fear and anxiety such a condition generates, with a phrase like "average expectable environment." As I said to you before, many of us who analyze so carefully the various subtleties of the developing conscious and unconscious mind in children and older people can miss a whole range of forces that affect the unconscious and the conscious—and can also miss a comprehension of what religion is about.

I believe that religious faith enables man to be free of himself, to find a destiny for himself that is outside of his own inevitably narrow sphere. To me the great danger in all political activity, not to mention professional activity, has to do with this kind of egoism—call it narcissism, call it the sin of pride that is in all of us, and is exploitable and that will exploit. We cannot completely rid ourselves of the kind of self-centeredness that is potentially destructive through more analysis, not five years of it, not ten years. But I do think a religious person like Simone Weil can spend a lifetime struggling against that self-centeredness (and its perhaps most malignant expression, self-righteousness) and succeed—and do so in a way that we have yet to understand. What for instance did she do with her brilliant mind, her fussiness, her cantankerousness, her pride, her chronic despair, her defiant self? I mean how did she wage a struggle with herself that had such significance? Her kind of struggle is an important one, not because a particular literary or political coterie deems that to be so, but because so many of us are faced with the kinds of agonies she faced. We seek after justice in the world; we look for a sense of our own particular distinctiveness; we feel a sense of outrage at the unnecessary pain so many millions of men and women experience. At the same time we realize, as she did, how we can as easily become an oppressor —oh, naturally, in the pursuit of what is right, just, and true. Simone Weil's greatest achievement as an intellectual, a political and moral philosopher, may have been her slowly realized and painfully stated distrust of her own mind's brilliance. She became increasingly skeptical of her capacity for symbolization, for dense theoretical display. Her eventual distrust of the mind's capacity for arrogance and coldness is what I think religious faith buttresses or ought to buttress. Man as himself subordinate to larger forces, to God, has to be reminded again and again (because he so very much wants to forget) how dangerously prideful he can become, how mean and vicious the best-educated minds, even well-analyzed minds, can turn out to be. I don't see in the writings of certain psychoanalytic theorists the kind of grace and humility that I find comes across in theologians, and which I particularly see in writers like Simone Weil—or Flannery O'Connor, to move to our country. I don't see in psychoanalytic theoreticians the kind of loveliness, the capacity for ambiguity and irony, that I find in Bernanos. So, I guess I feel sad, even as I know that my profession has a lot to offer people who are struggling and hurt and troubled. Having said that I immediately have to qualify myself—because it's not my *profession* that offers people anything, it's the particular individuals in it. And yet those individuals have learned something that is called "professional knowledge," which is what any profession offers to those men and women who get to call themselves a little ponderously and dangerously (the danger has to do with self-importance) "professional men" or "professional women." So these various abstractions and the "reality" they are meant to describe, amount to a tightrope, which each of us must walk upon. We have to acquire knowledge and skills, learn theory, join those institutions which promulgate and teach and instruct; and then we have to go and be on our own, depart for those lonely outposts which are an office, a clinic, a rectory, a confessional, which is any place where the suffering individual goes to the person of knowledge and is either healed— or, of course, made sicker and more hurt.

I look upon psychiatry and psychoanalysis as new elements in a tradition which goes back for centuries and centuries. As Erikson has pointed out again and again, our heirs are men like St. Augustine and Pascal, men who looked inward and struggled with themselves and somehow gained territory on themselves. I do not look upon us as proud scientists or the seers that we have become in a particular kind of culture, American culture. I think some of us are first-rate, compassionate and decent men, the difficulties of whose everyday work simply cannot be exaggerated. Some of us, however, are vulgar and obscene, are thoroughly allied with the rich and the powerful, are uncritical apologists for the status quo, are not worth paying much attention to—used as we are by various canny rhetoricians to justify various kinds of "realities" or to impugn the motives of young dissenters, while all the while we don't quite acknowledge our own motives, our willingness to ingratiate ourselves fearfully, yield submissively, so long as we continue to be respectable and favored and by no means short of cash.

Your question earlier about why we're not in jail is not very hard to answer. We, by and large, look upon ourselves as doctors —pure if not so simple. We are part of a profession which is a thoroughly prominent one, and many of us claim that, again, our work is "objective" or "value free" and without political dimensions to it. Our responsibility, as so many of us see it, is to see and talk with and help in so far as we can the particular people who define themselves as patients and come to us and ask us for help. And yet of course some of us feel that even there we have failed, because we see only *certain* people, and we fail to look at them and their lives as searchingly as we claim to do. Eager to understand the mind, we are not so eager to examine the political and economic forces at work upon the mind; nor have we done justice to the way the political arena, the marketplace, affect the child's sense of himself, the child's values, the child's way of talking and thinking, the expectations the child has about what his life or her life is going to be like in the future. Until we study and acknowledge such matters we really are not doing what we claim is our responsibility. Ironically, for all of his blind spots Freud was a political as well as an intellectual rebel; he had all sorts of thoroughly personal and also prickly ideas that alienated him from an entire society, an entire profession. But now he has become an icon, celebrated with statues and pictures, his words mulled over and chewed over— and why, one wonders. I suppose the answer is that so it goes in history. Those who place themselves on the shoulders of dissident leaders eventually become a respectable group of people who are hardly at the forefront of intellectual struggles. So we have become fat, well-off, of good reputation; and such people don't usually go to jail. In any event, I see no overwhelming reason for psychiatrists or psychoanalysts to be asked for their estimate of what constitutes or is "valid" about religious faith—and I say that even though I know how many psychiatrists have written about religious matters, and how steadfastly ministers and priests and rabbis, perhaps doubtful themselves, struggling hard and unsuccessfully for faith and belief, have turned to secular sources like us for a nod of support. The only sensible and sensitive job I have ever seen done on this subject has been Erikson's book on Luther, in which he explicitly refrains from interpreting psychoanalytically religious faith or religious doctrine or theological knowledge. Many others of us have shown how immodest we can be by taking on whole areas of human experience and labeling them, gratuitously at times, stupidly and meanly at other times, with all those choice new psychological expressions we have added to our everyday language.

One thing I know: I couldn't have done the work I did in the South without the "inner" sanctuary that churches can provide. And besides my personal desire to go to church and sit there and think and pray and sing and listen and feel touched and somehow more alive, I was constantly learning from blacks in the South and whites in Appalachia what religion can mean and be to people. I suppose I could say that I learned a lot about the mind of the poor—if one wants to get into that kind of abstraction, "the mind of the poor"—by going to church with poor blacks in the South and Appalachian whites in Kentucky and West Virginia. I learned a lot about how those men and women think and feel, and what the possibilities are for them, how they manage to survive, how they struggle and keep some of their wits about them. Yes, I learned those things right in church while listening and joining in; nor could I have learned from such people by sitting and asking "psychological" questions, questions aimed at "tapping their unconscious." As a matter of fact, I have seen in those people strengths, redemptive moments, that my particular mode of looking at them—the psychiatric and psychoanalytic mode—is simply not able to comprehend. We are experts at trying to fit into a theoretical body of knowledge certain kinds of complaints people have. We know less not only about human survival, but about human endurance—as I say, the redemptive possibilities in people, the way people grow, the way they struggle and overcome almost incomprehensible hazards and obstacles.

Berrigan: I want to return if possible to the question of Simone Weil—to what we could call the nature of modern religious experience. I remember reading recently in her diary (I think it is *Gravity and Grace*) that at several points she was struck with the intuition of, as she said, "putting on the universe for God." And she speaks of the body of this world as being the larger body of man himself, analogous to his corporal body. She seemed to have had, I would think, in the midst of her wish to transcend herself and to adore God this other sense of plunging into history and into mankind. Her whole spirit was distended, grievously, between those two realities, the reality of God and the reality of human suffering and human death; and she took part in both, embracing both. But I like not only the fact that she was in anguish personally as a woman who prayed to God, as a supplicant, but that she also connected her personal quest and struggle to the life and death experiences of the Nazi Occupation. And then there were those haunting, strange last days of hers, when she just about starved herself to death as a way of expressing her unity (across the miles and across her exile) with those under the Occupation. She took upon herself the world's suffering and died—and yet she has meant so much to some of us who are trying to work for a better kind of world.

Coles: In some lives the history of mankind becomes almost incarnate. It is very interesting: we talk as clinicians about "case histories," and we are always trying to give our patients an essentially historical sense of themselves. The questions we ask in our offices are historical questions. What was your past like? What did you do at five? What did you think at eight? What were the experiences you had x years ago? But we are not willing to go further, and dwell upon the psychological significance to our patients of that larger history which is also part of the individual's history—because, after all, American history lives on in every American child as a concrete fact of his or her growing up. My children are growing up in a certain way because certain things have happened in America over the years. I mean, my children are having their experiences with their mother and me—they live in a particular house in which my wife and I think and act in a certain way and thus affect the way our children think and act. But our children are also young Americans, which means they now have two hundred years of a certain kind of history behind them, and that history affects their lives every single day; affects what they do; affects what they think; affects what they plan; affects what they dream about; affects what their future is going to be; affects the way they get along with people, and with which people and under what sets of circumstances. Thus does larger history become the individual's history. I think the children and young men and women I worked with in the South in the sixties, when one phase of the civil rights struggle was taking place, knew what we are talking about. They weren't educated in psychiatric training centers, and they hadn't read Freud, but in their bones they knew they were in their lives joining individual action to historical change. In so doing, interestingly enough, they did very well. They surprised themselves (and certainly surprised me) with the strength and courage and persistence they mobilized, in spite of serious and sometimes almost inconceivable pressures. Perhaps they did so well, survived so hardily, because they had a chance to turn suffering into an achievement, a tangible social and political triumph. I have to contrast them with Simone Weil. Like her they were very conscious of what was going on all over the world but they were going uphill and she was going downhill, even as her world was going downhill and their world was going uphill.

I want to keep emphasizing this: when the black children I worked with in New Orleans and Atlanta talked about the efforts they were making as they desegregated schools in those cities, they made it clear to me that what they were doing was a psychological fact for them; they weren't only doing something historical, something for future Southern historians to write about or for political scientists to analyze. Simone Weil, for all the complexity of her thinking, would have easily understood the lean simplicity of those black children's remarks. What they all have in common, her and others who have struggled for social justice, is the direction they wanted their lives to take—a direction which made their so-called "personal" lives mean something to others as well, others who would be grateful for what they said or did. Simone Weil felt called upon, as indeed the sit-in leaders were called upon, the freedom riders were called upon, to find out for herself and those around her, insofar as she could, what it is to live close to history. Now I saw a little girl in New Orleans do the same thing—and talk about her efforts with the drawings or little compositions that she gave me. She tried to set down on paper what it meant to be at a turning point in the black man's American experience and what it did to her, what she felt. She wrote as Simone Weil wrote. She wrote as someone who felt history quite nearby. I think that for some reason we doctors don't want our patients to think about such issues, because we have isolated ourselves from history. We too often talk as if everything begins with Freud. We don't want to know about Kierkegaard. We don't want to know about St. Augustine. We don't want to know about Nietzsche or Schopenhauer and what they have to say about the mind and the struggles and tensions that plague the mind. So, being somewhat ahistorical ourselves, being prideful and overly preoccupied with a certain body of knowledge, we exclude ourselves from other currents of knowledge, whether they be philosophical or theological. We don't think of political developments, or social and economic developments as psychological forces. We are at the mercy of our narrowness. Simone Weil for us becomes one more "neurotic." Her "obsessions" interest us clinically—and meanwhile we ignore her challenge to us as persons. Under such circumstances we naturally would fail to comprehend what Faulkner comprehended—the endurance of black people, their capacity to deal with the most overwhelming kinds of stresses in ways that are not only dignified but (the best word I can find) redemptive.

Berrigan: Do you hesitate to use that word?

Coles: I fear that there were a number of important words and ideas I somehow didn't think much about when I was learning to be a psychiatrist. When I was taking my training in child psychiatry I was asked by a young boy I was treating who happened to be black if I would come to his home, to visit his home. I told my supervisor that, and asked what to do about it. Well I was immediately asked *why* the boy asked that of me, what his request *meant*. Was the child perhaps trying to "manipulate" me, "control" me, get me to do things for *this* reason and *that* reason? And on my side, what was I doing, what "technical" error was I making, for the child even to ask such a question? We went over and over the matter in the legalistic way that supervisors and supervisees so often do. Only now do I realize how thoughtless and self-centered the two of us were, how uptight and bound to our own way of seeing things and doing things. The child was really telling me that if I really wanted to understand him I would have to see his world; I would have to understand what housing is like in a ghetto, what he and his parents as black people had to face, what they had had to face all along, as they lived in South Carolina and then in Boston. I wasn't interested in any of that; I didn't even stop and think about such matters. (It was the late 1950s, and we had no "race problem" then!) I wanted to know why the child was having a "learning block" in school. And a "learning block" is something that for me, then, had to do with an Oedipal family almost abstract in nature; that is, not tied to the particular social and economic and racial elements in a child's life, but only to his mother's and father's "relationship" with him and his "relationship" with them—as if such "relationships" ever exist in a social or economic or racial vacuum, a historical void. So I think Simone Weil was onto something about not only history but our deepest psychological needs. She was onto the "relationship" between an individual life and the moment of history in which that life is lived, and particularly she was onto the relationship between those "spiritual pioneers" who are especially sensitive to the bridges which connect history and life history. She may well have been a cannier psychologist or psychiatrist than most of us.

Berrigan: She presents us with a fascinating puzzle. On the one hand she was suspicious, as you have mentioned, of almost every possible political alignment or ideological position; and on the other hand, she demonstrated a very mysterious but organic or spiritual unity with others. It seems to me that she expresses in a rather exemplary way the struggle practically every modern person wages with alienation. I could say wages *against* alienation, but I mean *with* it, with the inescapable reality of it. We can be only so close to family or religion or culture. We can take only so much part in the continuing conflicts which go to make up history. Yet, we have a need to do so, to link arms with others, and I mean not only our neighbors but others in history whose sacrifices have given us much to fall back on. Nor was she content to link arms symbolically or intellectually. She loved books. She loved Plato and the Greeks; but she wanted to be part of the struggle her own countrymen were making. And strangely enough, she supplies us with an example, a metaphor almost, of where and how that "link" can be accomplished. We have the metaphor of prison, and in her case we have the metaphor of exile, and maybe the two are not that far apart. For her it was important to be a certain kind of exile; she was in England and yet she chose to die rather than to luxuriate in exile or rather than to use exile as an excuse for further alienation from her people, further spiritual distance from suffering. It seems to me that she turned totally and consumedly in the other direction and in the end died with the conviction that she was one with those workers she loved, those occupied and conquered people who were so much on her mind, and whom her soul reached out to with such passion.

Coles: Speaking of Simone Weil's exile, are you perhaps trying to stake out for yourself an alternative which is both personal and historical? I mean, you have chosen to be a fugitive—and in your case that means you are willing to go through the difficulty and pain your present situation imposes, and you are willing to remove yourself from a particular relationship to society you have up to now enjoyed. I presume you want to do so because you feel you cannot bow to the government's wishes. Yet you are not a lawbreaker of long standing; you have not exactly lived the life of a confidence man or a criminal. I would imagine you are trying desperately to weigh the dangers of breaking a law and the dangers of silence or only token (or "manageable") opposition to a state of affairs one considers an outrage and a scandal. When does the individual have an obligation to assert himself in such a way that he makes a public statement about his country's policies? What are the limits to protest—when the protesters feel things getting worse and feel they have done all they can by marching in parades or writing to their congressmen? You have heard those questions asked before—by me and others before me. I merely mention them now because the answers you seem to have come up with place you in substantial spiritual jeopardy—or so Simone Weil would no doubt say, and not necessarily without sympathy.

Berrigan: I think I have at least some idea what she meant when she talked about the experience of rejection and alienation, when she talked about the acceptance of exile—but then at the same time went on to assert a very powerful sense of solidarity with others, with all of her countrymen. As for myself, I don't know how to explain in detail my present position. I know this, though: I am trying with all my heart and soul to move closer to the realities of history, the realities which millions of people have to face in their everyday lives. I may now be an exile within my own country, but I feel that I have been trying in what I have done to speak for others as well as myself, and to embrace across the world many who are undergoing what I take to be struggles which are related to mine. I am trying to say clumsily something that I think is very simple: I have a sense that the future of man lies not with the pretensions of the White House or the Kremlin, but in those very small and humiliated nodes of light which are to be found all over the world, including our own country, but which perhaps exist most poignantly and strikingly in the so-called Third World, where suffering is so universally experienced, where memories of colonialism are so recent, and where unusual people arise almost in the nature of things. I still feel I am not being clear, though. Maybe one cannot speak about such matters without becoming complicated. Anyway, I think there is something important to be undergone, something with a certain spiritual value to it; it is almost as if to be cast out can become a way of being cast in, which means I will taste not solely or even primarily the bitterness of being an American locked up, such as my brother, or an American on the run, but I will also taste a fate millions of others know, millions of people whose historical struggle matters very much, even if not to those who run our military machine and plan our foreign policy and invest money in the semicolonial countries we still dominate in various parts of the world. I can only speak tentatively about this, but I do have the sense that being in some serious human trouble in this society is a very important geography right now for trying to discern what the future is going to be; and by the same token to be in no trouble at all is to share in what I take to be a frightening movement toward violence and death. To resist that movement is one's choice.

Coles: I do not see our situation in this country as starkly (even apocalyptically) as you do. I am interested, though, in the implications of what you just said. Those who want to fight deathlike conformity and learn about both themselves and the world may have to take risks they find unacceptable. Perhaps if one really wants to find out about oneself one has to become unsettled in a truly significant and continuing way—as Freud certainly knew. But I question whether one can find out all there is to know about oneself psychologically by free associating in an office, in a private office at thirty or forty dollars an hour. I mean, what one misses in that kind of guided introspection is just too vast. The whole tone of one's life as it is lived in the world, politically and economically and socially and historically, simply does not come across in that kind of analysis, and if we want to know all there is that is going on in the mind (and I mean by that as much as we can know—obviously we can never know everything) then it seems to me that we have to look for new places in which such knowledge can be discovered. After all, when Freud set up that office of his and devised the couch, he was also locating himself and his patients in what you would call a new geographical position; and a very redemptive position it was for those who had never gone to people like him before, had never before been treated as Freud treated them, never been given the kind of respect, the kind of revolutionary respect he offered to those so-called neurotics in turn-of-thecentury Vienna. Now it may just be that new geographers will have to help us obtain the kind of freedom and self-awareness we want and need today—this being seventy years after 1900 and this being not Vienna but the United States of America.

Berrigan: My brother and I have talked to a lot of people over the two years in which we were under appeal—and we urged them not to follow us in a literal minded way, but look to their own situation, and then act accordingly. We were trying to reduce the chasm that exists in most lives between what we have called awareness on the one hand and on the other *action* —and I mean action that responds to the mind's intelligence and the heart's "reasons" Pascal wrote about. My brother and I

have wanted, as Phil puts it, to "share our lives." And it is interesting, I think, and very profound on his part, that he calls *that*
the revolution—sharing one's life with others. Now, is there a
difference in that kind of "sharing" and what goes on between a
psychiatrist and a patient, or a priest in the confessional and a
person who comes to see him? I think so. It seems to me that if
we are to "share our lives" as Phil and I hope to do, we have to
share ourselves not only with each other but with the world;
the horror of war, the horror of racism, these become very personal matters, and propel us *outward,* away from those private
and pleasant and satisfying and "supportive" encounters which
too often help people "forget about" the world's tragedies, and
so feel, ultimately, indifferent to them. The world becomes a
"third party"—an annoying "interference," so to speak. Do you
see what I mean? In so many of my discussions with students—
with young Catholics in the late fifties—we settled difficulties
in their lives by talking together, just the two of us—and in a
way, I now see, we didn't even touch upon so many things, let
alone "settle" them.

Coles: Yes, I think I see your point. In psychiatry, too, we so
often want to exclude the world. Many of us have gone to absurd extremes to do so. We won't put certain things on our
office walls, because they reveal to the patient things about
ourselves. We darken our offices, the patients come in, they lie
down, they close their eyes, they have "associations," we inter-
pret them, and the whole drift of the hour gets them away from
the world, removes them from outside "distractions," so that they
can have a certain *private* kind of experience with us. Within
limits I can go along with some of that: people have their various nightmares, and they need to *concentrate* on finding out
what is wrong and why. But the outside world lives in our every
bone and muscle—and affects how things go even in the most
cloistered rooms. And some of our patients get the notion that a
kind of ultimate reality is the kind of reality they experience in
our offices. They want to focus on their "problems" to the ex-
clusion of their "activities"; they even lose interest in *doing*—

all they want to do is analyze, analyze themselves. Now certain individuals do indeed need to stop and take a look, a long look at themselves and their behavior, but it is an illusion for them to think that life itself ought to be lived that way—with endless self-consciousness and detachment. Nor are some patients (and their doctors) able to avoid turning their preoccupations into weapons; anyone "unanalyzed" is looked down upon, treated as somehow a lesser person. Again, the illusion—an illusion with no future, I might add—is that a particular kind of private (therapeutic) encounter will satisfy the person's various existential dilemmas, perhaps by replacing them with the infinite demands of "analysis."

Berrigan: I find a very strange kind of resonance in what you've said with my own experience. I am talking about "sacramental confession" or "regular confession"—that is, the one-to-one relationship in a confessional. You know in recent years, as the Church has changed, less and less Catholics are presenting themselves for that sacrament, and at the same time more and more Catholics are trying to find ways of celebrating the Eucharist together. It's not that people still don't feel various guilts and a sense of moral failure before God and the community. Rather, young people especially don't find confession a suitable way of expressing such feelings. They don't want to go into darkness and talk into the ear of one man. What they are looking for, it seems to me, can be called a socialization of conscience. They want a social expression of the sacrament, a renewal on their part to the community—as one of its members who has been delinquent and is seeking readmission through confession of fault and through the forgiveness of the whole community. I don't want to push this too far, because I think on certain occasions a one-to-one relationship can be very important.

Coles: And very rewarding.

Berrigan: But the fact is that for a long time many of us had observed that the one-to-one sacramental exchange actually

worked toward the alienation of conscience rather than its education or its further imbedding in the reality of the world. We
could hear hundreds and hundreds of confessions over a period
of years, as I did, and remember on the fingers of one hand the
persons who had ever spoken to us about racism or wars and the
everyday social and economic injustice one *ought* to notice
and as a Christian work against.

Coles: We are educated not to think of certain things as sin-
ful; they are simply what *is*, what the world is *like*.

Berrigan: Yes. And ironically, when one is allowed to "confess," but is not (as in a more communal situation) asked to confront these issues and face them with others—then, of all things,
one's isolation and indifference, one's sinfulness, is strengthened,
rather than "forgiven," hence presumably diminished.

Coles: By the same token patients who go to psychiatrists
have been educated not to think of some of these social problems
as things to discuss with a doctor—namely, the way they hate
other people, the way they exploit others. How often do patients
come to clinics worried about their racial prejudices, their re-
sentment of various groups of people, their wish to destroy
whole nations or to see their country destroy another country?
One would think that such ideas and wishes and hates consti-
tute a very profound kind of psychological difficulty. But those
are not the difficulties we have been educated to look upon as
"problems" in need of help or "analysis." One doesn't get *that*
analyzed. One doesn't try to get rid of *that*. Nor do many doctors even try to ask their patients the kinds of questions that
would highlight such ways of thinking, and hopefully challenge them—as we challenge other "phobias" or "anxieties" or
"rivalries" in those who come to see us. We don't look upon
those matters as our domain. Those are "social problems," those
are for the sociologists to ask people about.

Berrigan: One thinks about how Lyndon Johnson went off to
pray during the night before he decided to begin bombing
North Vietnam. I think that that is one of the most extraordinary

and instructive things I have heard in the last ten years. It says so much about religion, about that man's soul, about his expectation from prayer, and—at least it seems to me—it says much about our churches that he would return from an experience like that clothed in a kind of divine approval for the murder of people in cities. He not only was convinced that it was the good American thing to do; he believed he was blessed, given Christ's sanction to go ahead and press all those buttons in his big office. One would want to laugh contemptuously—if the matter were not so awful and obscene and tragic.

7 • "Twice-Born Men"

Berrigan: Someone in a recent article on the New York Black Panthers (a man who watched them in a courtroom day after day) finally referred to this group of young black people as "twice-born men." The expression stuck with me for many reasons—and maybe one reason had to do with my own present struggle to understand what I think you would call "the truth of my life." I don't really know how to describe the major influences on my thinking. The Bible means so very much to me— but so do the writings of those men and women who are struggling in this century against various oppressors. I acknowledge in myself the kind of utopianism Camus would call "modest" and "embodied." I suppose I should go back to the imagery we mentioned earlier: one walks on a high wire and tries to balance a certain long-range vision of what is ideal and to be hoped for— as against the harsh and limiting realities of daily experience. The question of what is possible for human beings it seems to me is one way of looking at the rack on which the world is stretching us day after day. We see intense suffering and at the same time we see very real changes for the good in the hearts of many people.

Then I continue to be haunted by the Church and its destiny —and by the meaning of the sacraments as that meaning has changed over the centuries. You will remember that the sacramental rite of baptism was originally conceived to mark the adult's passage from one world of values to a community of radically different values. After all, these rites of passage did not arise in a vacuum; they arose in the nightmarish atmosphere which is conveyed to us by John in the Book of Revelations, and which concerned, as far as we can discover, a despised minority's confrontation with Caesarean power, imperial power, warmaking power by the necessity of things. So, John, in that first generation after Jesus, is forced to face, with his community, exactly what believers ought to do in such a situation—where it was not an abstract question of worshiping the true God or worshiping Caesar as god, because Caesar's demands for adulation were expressed very concretely: membership in the armed forces, participation in wars of conquest. That being the case, one who entered the Christian community in those first years of its existence did so as an act of faith—and with the sure knowledge that he faced trial and death as a traitor who refused to cooperate with the government. And so far as we can piece it together from John's surreal visions it appears as though a question was asked and an answer demanded of the community amid the very concrete and dense circumstances of their lives as subjects of that Roman Empire. They were forced by the very exigencies of their faith to answer no. Then, according to Paul, what emerged from the waters of that rite of passage, that commitment by a community of believers, was a newborn man or woman. That is to say, those adults had entered with very open eyes upon a way that was radically different from the way of paganism, a way they considered not only superior but for which they were willing, quite fervently willing, to sacrifice their human bodies. It was a truly astonishing kind of decision.

Paul also draws very heavily upon the first couple of chapters of Genesis—the introduction of violence into the garden; he could not overlook the historical struggle between Cain and Abel and the disobedience of their parents. Very strikingly and very deliberately he indicates that the fruit of disobedience is almost immediately human violence. And he did not have in mind just random violence, but the fraternal violence of brother against brother, which can of course become brother nation against brother nation or brother "people" against brother "people." That reading of the story of Genesis was crucial in the development of the rite of the sacrament. The story of Cain and Abel was read as a forecast of the struggle between man's violence and the example of Christ. One is confronted, so to speak, by the companionship of Cain and his stigma on the one hand and on the other the mark of Christ which he forever offers us—a sign of *the* way.

I don't want to bother you with the still unsettled theological questions that I find knocking on my mind's door in the middle of the night these days—as I struggle to make sense of Mr. J. Edgar Hoover and Mr. John Mitchell and the rest of them. I mean, exactly who are they? Henchmen of a Roman Emperor? Grandsons of Cain? Kind and loving disciples of Jesus Christ our Lord? And apart from them, I keep wondering what is possible for human beings. In my recent experience I see things converging constantly across the lines of "culture" and "religion" and "ethnic background" into a common assumption, held by many, that we either enter into a profound form of nonviolent humanitarianism, or we become part of the proliferating problem, as Cleaver would put it—having refused to become part of the solution.

Coles: The issue of what is possible in people is something that intrigues me. A few years ago I read Malcolm X's autobiography, in which he described his utterly brutal childhood. His father was killed when he was a child, his mother was driven to madness. He knew extreme poverty and hardship. As a clinician I have known so many people from comfortable, upper middle class homes who have sought out psychiatrists because they are in despair, troubled beyond their own comprehension, and indeed often enough thoroughly paralyzed. Yet Malcolm X somehow not only survived a bleak and frantic and near-chaotic childhood, but wrote a moving and sensitive book about his life, including his early years. And more significantly, he was a man who in his last years was being reborn, to use your imagery. I mean, he was going through a profound spiritual crisis. He was becoming a spiritual leader toward the end. Anyone who calls himself a child psychiatrist ought to ask: whence this? What in Malcolm X's life enabled that kind of development? I am not only referring to the peculiar tenacity a suffering and vulnerable person can develop within himself or herself. I have in mind the genuine thoughtfulness and compassion and sensitivity which gradually evolved in the short life of this man. Perhaps he is a model of the "new man" you mention—an example of what is possible in people. Out of his prison experience, out of his devastating childhood, out of all the sadness and pain he went through in one ghetto after another, he could somehow build more than a "life" for himself. He found the resources for spiritual growth—to the point that many of us, less "disadvantaged" and "deprived," can only scratch our heads and wonder what do *we* lack, why have *we* become so cautious and restricted and cravenly self-satisfied.

Was Malcolm X so very unusual? Of course he was unusual; he was a leader. But for years I have seen in the South and in Appalachia and in the ghettos of the North poor and desperate people who manage to find for themselves large stretches of intelligence and discrimination—in the best sense of the word discrimination. They are people who are very hard pressed, who often go hungry, who are sick and persecuted and in constant trouble of one kind or another; and yet they are able to demonstrate not only humor and liveliness, but the kinds of "ethical concern" I think those of us in the universities and the divinity schools talk about—but don't always ourselves summon. Now we social scientists often fail to take note of or comment upon those qualities in the children of the poor—in blacks and in Appalachian whites, for example. Instead we talk endlessly about the "disadvantage" and "deprivation" of the poor. The poor are indeed disadvantaged (quite literally they are); and certainly they are deprived of certain things they desperately need. Nor ought they to be romanticized. Their difficulties are serious and sometimes stunting. And yet I see in many impoverished families I work with a concern for one another that is remarkable. And I hear among those "illiterate" men and women and children a capacity for philosophical and theological speculation that rivals anyone's. They ask over and over why they are here, what they ought do, what they must do —and not least, what they might do, given different circumstances. Among them, too, live the "twice born," the "new men."

Now you asked a moment ago what is possible for people. In the fifties the President of the United States said we cannot have changes in our society until there are changes in people. We cannot have changes, for instance, in our laws, changes that would affect the way the races get along, until the hearts of people change, said Eisenhower. And yet when laws *are* changed and then enforced rigorously, people also change; they respond to new legal and social and political realities. White Southerners I worked with once told me *never;* they said they would never go along with school desegregation. But they did, and quickly. Of course when a national administration backtracks and implies or subtly suggests that recent changes need not be maintained, then people go back to their old ways.

There is nothing surprising in what I am saying; I think we all know that people accommodate themselves rather readily to changing historical circumstances—perhaps *too* readily. What we know is that there are all kinds of possibilities in people; there are all kinds of qualities that can emerge, given an enabling historical moment, given the encouragement a society offers. There is also, I fear, in most of us a large capacity for violence. Nor is "education" any panacea in this regard. What we are haunted by is the example in this century of one of the most "educated" and "advanced" nations in the world running amok.

They didn't need Head Start programs in Germany in the twenties. The Germans were well educated by and large. They had produced a fine culture over many decades. And yet, given economic chaos and social unrest an entire nation could be led into heinous crimes. I do not believe—I know the matter is indeed arguable—that what happened was the specific result of German culture or Germany's peculiar philosophical and social traditions. I believe that any nation, given sufficient economic and social injustice, can become increasingly seized by violence and chaos, hence be ripe for one or another murderous demagogue—and their ideologies (Left versus Right) seem to be less important than their common brutishness.

As for individuals, Lord knows I see patients every day who are hurt and troubled people. But over a period of weeks and months one sees in them not only the *desire* for health, but the continuing presence of health which cannot for various reasons find a way of expression—but health which nevertheless is there and waiting, as it were. And so I would almost get religious, and say that I don't believe anyone, anyone at all, is ultimately beyond some kind of saving moment—given what is needed to bring about or enable that "moment." And I would say that even about people some of us dismiss as awful or hopeless or evil or sick—and in this regard there are so many different kinds of words we have. I worked with members of the Klu Klux Klan in the South even as I was working with black families. They were racists, they were hurt and troubled men and women, and their children of course were infected·with virulent hatreds; and yet I saw even in some of those families a wide range of possibilities, virtues, difficulties, tragedies. And I wonder at times whether some of the negative things people have to face are not potentially of great value, because tragedies and difficulties often can herald growth—something which novelists and playwrights have known long before those who call themselves experts in child development came on the scene. One man, a member of the Klu Klux Klan, said to me after I had come to know him for some length of time that he thought his life might have been a different life had America been a different country when he was growing up. Now when a man who is an unashamed and rather voluble bigot can tell me (not in any propagandistic or moralistic or analytic way, and not particularly in a self-conscious way, but almost in an offhand and casual way) that he might have been a different person if the state of Louisiana had been different and if America had been different, he is telling me something about the nature of society and its relationship to the individual, and he is telling me an important psychological truth, one which I am not so sure someone like me is always ready to comprehend. He is really telling me that at any given moment anyone *is* not only what he has *come to be*, but what he *might have been*. Each of us carries within himself (living in us even if not available or apparent) all kinds of resources and possibilities—and some of them may be hidden and known to no one, including the particular person in question. Now I'm not talking about the "unconscious" *per se;* I am saying that people can suddenly organize and bring together qualities they either vaguely sense in themselves, or don't stop and think about, or do think about, but have in the past dismissed—all because the world "outside" has suddenly said *yes* rather than *no* or *now* rather than *later*.

I worked in New Orleans a decade ago; there I watched mobs form around little black children going into white schools. A year later I went up to Atlanta and saw no mobs at all form when black children there went into white schools. Fascinatingly enough, the first questions I got when I went to talk about those experiences at medical and psychiatric meetings were these: what kind of people would join a mob, and what kind of psychopathy and psychopathology would prompt people to heckle children and be violent on the street, and what kind of treatment did those people need, since they were obviously quite disturbed? Of course one had to point out that there were no mobs in Atlanta. Does that mean the "mental health" of Atlanta's people was better? Does that mean Atlanta's citizens are of sounder mind than New Orleans's citizens? Well, of course not.

What it means is that the city of Atlanta at a particular moment in American history would not allow a mob to form. The city of Atlanta (for its own various and mixed reasons—commercial reasons, moral reasons, reasons that had to do with the "image" of the city) could tell thousands and thousands of people, not in an explicit and didactic way but in vague and indirect ways: look, cool it, refrain from behaving in certain ways, don't take to the streets, don't lose your tempers, and don't even try to start trouble—because it won't be sanctioned or tolerated. I think such "exchanges" go on all the time. By that I mean we constantly take our cues from the world we live in. And if there is forthright moral leadership in that world people often respond to such leadership, despite their past "positions" or "attitudes." I don't see us as reflexic products of particular psychological drives, limited by certain kinds of "problems," and able to change only after years of "treatment." Parents know what is possible for their children—and often enough for them as mothers and fathers: a hundred different directions can be taken by children, given support here or, of course, disapproval there —and on and on.

A good example of what I am trying to say has been provided us not by a psychiatrist but by a historian—in C. Vann Woodward's book on Tom Watson. It seems to me Tom Watson's life shows in microcosm what happens to all of us. When an inherently idealistic and loving man is continually thwarted and denied and cheated and robbed and insulted, eventually he turns to hate and becomes violent and mean toward others. So it happened with Tom Watson, and so it happens with us today, millions of us. All of us struggle to find out what opportunity we can have for a more loving and affectionate way of getting along with ourselves and others—only to meet up not only with the indifference of the world but the deceit and the brutality. I'm talking about institutionalized meanness and brutality—which as part of our "outer" world we all have to live with and come to terms with, and which children at seven and eight know about and have comprehended and have already begun to accept and take for granted and (most horrible to watch developing) as a matter of fact take in as part of their "inner" world.

I hear it said that there's just *so* much you can do with people. I hear it said that people are the way they are, and they can't change overnight, can't be born again; rather, it takes years, it takes generations. One can only say in reply that there is an enormous amount of evidence—historical, psychological, clinical, psychiatric and psychoanalytic—which tells us people *are* many things and can *become* many things. Again, I go back to Malcolm X as an example of this, or in a different way, Tom Watson, or the member of the Klan I just mentioned. I think that when St. Paul talked about the "new man" or the "twice born" he was trying to say that we don't have to be what we once were, and that we can be more than we presently are, and that every day (even every minute) of our lives offers us a chance—to demonstrate our ability to move, walk, gain territory on ourselves, realize for ourselves a certain coherence, a certain spirit of openness and concern. What really makes a difference in our lives is not only what we were driven to when we were young or what we experienced at such and such an age, although yes, those are terribly significant matters. What we *are* is a function of so many things: accidents, incidents, things that are unpredictable and that yet have become the most important things in our lives—things like whom we meet at one or another point in time, or things like what happened in the world this year or the next year, things like where we were when we encountered someone. We all know that; we all know we met our wives or husbands because of this accident or because we just happened to be doing that. So our lives become profoundly, crucially changed because we admired a teacher or camp counselor we only happened (we *chanced*) to spend time with, or because we by luck met someone here or there who later became a friend, a wife, a husband—well, I shouldn't keep on saying the obvious. If such decisive moments can happen in all of our lives, how much *more* could happen, might happen, if people were to come together and make it their business to *want* certain things to happen, want an atmosphere to exist in which change is possible, in which events keep taking place and in that way encouraging us to take notice and learn, and again, change.

Berrigan: It seems to me that what you are saying is quite subversive in its implications.

Coles: I feel myself talking common sense.

Berrigan: Well, then, subversive common sense. At times I feel this society is becoming a kind of Manichaean madhouse— in which so many of us are being frozen, whether it be the Klan or the Mafia or the Weathermen or indeed my brother and myself; frozen into definitions which declare us enemies of goodness or irredeemably evil or objects of a manhunt. It seems to me that the master metaphor in our society these days, always lurking in the background, is the metaphor of modern war, whether it be cold or hot. That is to say, our society declares itself good and virtuous in principle and declares others (minorities within the nation and various countries on the several continents) to be the enemy. We don't want to "live and let live"; we want to dominate. In comparison, I was struck recently by the example of a liberal minister in the South who deliberately would seek out Klansmen and try to talk with them, be with them, understand them; and especially he would seek them out when they were in legal jeopardy. He would spend time with them.

Coles: I know him: Will Campbell. He is an extraordinary man indeed.

Berrigan: Yes. Once he went to see a Klansman just before he went off to prison. I believe the minister was trying to say that the hunter and the hunted, the respectable burgher and the exiled man or poor man or racially different man have got to look at one another as fellow human beings, as people who *care* for each other in spite of differences, rather than want to kill each other. One of the things that Christianity at least here and there and now and then can do is to do exactly what Will Campbell did; that is to say, the Christian (if he follows Christ's example) will constantly want to cross over and be with the excommunicated, or be with the stigmatized, or be with the so-called "enemy." In that spirit, Howard Zinn and I decided we were going to Hanoi—for the sake of both sides. We didn't believe that enmities could be arbitrarily and intransigently decreed. We felt we had a right to our own ideas about other human beings. We felt we had an obligation to meet people being called our foes and come to know them, even if Lyndon Baines Johnson said they deserve from us only thousands of bombs. We went to Vietnam not as enemies of America, nor as enemies of the Vietnamese; we went to the Vietnamese as fellow human beings who abhor violence, be it committed by large nations or small nations, our nation or other nations. I think the same spirit ought be demonstrated by all of us toward the Panthers and toward the Weathermen. When we become pursuers, people on a collective manhunt, we enter into a moral stalemate, which is destructive to lives, and just as important, destructive to our spiritual substance.

Coles: Christ eagerly challenged us in many ways, and one important way was this: he asked us to forsake a pharisaic view of human nature which is flat and single-minded, which constantly sets up niches and categories, totes up sums, adds, subtracts, looks at people with a view to checking them off, labeling them, oh so strictly defining them. Christ said no; He insisted that there are dozens and dozens of possibilities in all of us, so we simply cannot be fitted into an accountant's language, even a theological accountant's language. He declared that anyone can be saved; and He reminded us that there is an ineffable and mysterious quality to how salvation comes about. When Christ emphasized free grace, He emphasized (through the example of His own life) that growth comes through suffering, that pain and hardship and even exile are not necessarily things to be avoided, and that disapproval, even profound rejection, by the majority of the powerful ones in a society can be quite compatible with spiritual growth, He was attacking the notion that a particular elect has the right to spell out what we think or do —and indeed define our destiny. Needless to say, one era's outcasts can become the next era's heroes, as history has shown, including Christian history. Christ and His followers, however despised and scorned and ignored by Pharisees and generals and prominent officials of one kind or another emerged as, after all, people who were growing, who were blessed, who were the sign of a new age, who were becoming born again. Now I would suggest that many of us who struggle clinically with patients have got to think about such matters. We, too, see people who look down upon themselves and often enough have been looked down upon by others. If we concentrate only on the negative side of such people, they seem almost hopeless—or as we would have it, incurable. Again, we ought to remember that what matters is not the letter, but the spirit, not what a generation's smug, self-satisfied Pharisees say, but what the forgotten and forsaken might become.

Berrigan: Speaking of elites (and man's history has been marked by successive struggles against various elites) one of the results of the Manichaean impasse we've been discussing is not merely that a lot of helpless people are destroyed or lost to their potential, but that it becomes more and more difficult to judge the judges. Who is to examine the FBI and its leadership and its ethos? How lawful and ethical and Christian was Lyndon Baines Johnson? I remember at the time of our trial, in one very hot exchange, the judge kept insisting again and again that no American could for any reason break a law and expect immunity from the consequences. And one of our defendants said quite simply, "And your statement, Your Honor, applies also to the President?" And at that point there was great disarray. The judge could only say—I quote exactly as I remember: "Well, you understand, it's hard to apply what I said to his case." And the response of the defendant was, "And that is what this trial is all about." I think that the poor are held legally accountable for just about everything they do, whereas the powerful get away with murder—and sometimes (I fear) literally do. Indeed one wonders whether some of our powerful politicians and generals will *ever* be called to account for their various mistakes—and crimes. The crimes our so-called statesmen commit are veiled, denied, paid for in the blood of thousands of innocent men, women and children of this and other nations. So it goes—what is called "politics." We fostered the so-called Nuremburg Rules or Principles against the Nazis, but who is to stop us and ask us whether our leaders also don't need to be "evaluated" by some high court. For those who belong to the radical religious community, I don't care whether it is located in the East or West, whether it is Christian or Buddhist, there is a constant insistence that man stands before the transcendent eye of God as he stands before the judgment of his community, no matter what range of power he holds; and furthermore, whatever judgments are rendered, they are not retributive so much as (in purpose) redemptive. Mercy is the point. We are trying to say even to those who in the name of law or in the name of power commit the most awful actions against others—we are declaring those people redeemable too, simply because they also stand under God's laws. Nor can such "distinguished" people exempt themselves, in the name of whatever "position" or "resources" they have come upon, from the fact that all men are naked finally, that all men need to be saved—perhaps ultimately from their ego, their self-idolatry.

Coles: People like you are considered by many people "way out," and "irrelevant" to the lives of millions and millions of Americans—our so-called middle class people, our white lower middle class. Your sympathies are so different from theirs that one hears it argued you are condemned by your acts and ideas to the smallest and most parochial of audiences—because the vast majority of people are loyal to America, loyal to American traditions, support the President, and want us out of Vietnam, yes, but as winners not losers. The distinction is between two groups: one is small and heretical; one is large and generally conformist and in agreement with things as they are.

Well, I have worked for five years with so-called lower middle class white families in Boston and its suburban towns—and I started doing my work long before subjects like "the white backlash" or the patriotic activities of the "hard hats" became front-page news. I started doing my work because I was interested in how black children who were bussed from a ghetto got along with white kids in suburban schools or in lower middle class schools within the city limits. Actually, I've always been interested in what white children think about black children. (In the South I worked with children of both races.) In any event I think many of us do these white working class men and women a grave injustice. Some politicians who claim to speak for the "ordinary man," the "forgotten American," can be condescending and arrogant in the way they exhort the very people they claim to speak for. It is true, one can go to a home—a policeman's home, a fireman's home, a blue-collar worker's home, a white-collar worker's home—and hear all kinds of prejudicial remarks, all kinds of narrow loyalties espoused, hatreds espoused; but one can hear other things, too. One can hear a sense of outrage at the inequalities in our society, a sense of bitterness at the way workers are treated by corporations, a sense of hurt and pain that reflects the ethical concern and moral outrage people feel and carry with them all through their lives—and have to push aside in their struggles to make the next dollar. Yes, people die; they forget or forcibly push aside their better selves, become disenchanted, lose hope, turn into the caricatures that our politicians portray and pander to and try to egg on, all so that votes will be gained, power secured. But what gets ignored in all of this is a whole range of ideas and beliefs so many of our people have, but don't easily talk about in public. I have heard policemen and firemen and construction workers and factory workers and gas station attendants and bank tellers and postal clerks rail against lying and tricky politicians, and the exploitation of people at the hands of insensitive and thoughtless corporations. I have heard those same men recall the struggles they remember their fathers and mothers and grandfathers and grandmothers having under an oftentimes unfair social and economic and political system. When we talk about "silent Americans," *those* are some things a lot of Americans keep under their hats, keep silent about, because they are afraid to talk openly about "controversial" issues. I have yards (miles it seems) of tapes to prove that what is "silent" in them is a good deal of social criticism, a good number of canny observations about who owns and runs this society, a good amount of latent idealism. What I said about that Klan member applies to millions and millions of Americans —who also might be different, might speak and act differently, were this a differently organized and inspired society.

Berrigan: So many people in America have given up in recent decades because their possibilities had never really been pointed out to them and encouraged. I think what we witness today is a constant effort—the poisonous tone is set from above—to declare that certain people are such and such, whether they be called middle Americans or Panthers. If they are *only* such and such, they are forbidden the change that is possible to them. To call people a "silent" group is to condemn them to accept the state of silence, which means they'll never expect a rational or courageous or enlightened speech from their leaders.

Coles: This is a democracy, yet I am sure some of our politicians feel most comfortable when most citizens are indeed silent —and obliging and unquestioning and willing to take this one's explanations or someone else's "policy." We need others to confirm our own moral ambiguities. We need others to confirm our power.

Berrigan: I have wished recently I might be able to establish some contact with the Weathermen, who are also underground. I would want to do so in an effort to declare (across all sorts of distances and differences) my solidarity with at least a certain side of them, the side appalled by the lies and deceits so many of us fearfully and uncritically accept. The Weathermen have been stereotyped as subhuman, as irredeemably violent, as animals on the run. I would be trying to find out what has brought them to their present situation, what has occurred to them in their community since they went underground, and whether or not they have wanted to reconsider some of their past (and inflammatory) statements with regard to other human beings—reconsider their openly declared disrespect for human life. I suspect that the Weathermen are not all of a piece, do not lack great moral and spiritual conflicts, and may well be trying to grow and change. Similarly with the Panthers. I often wonder whether some of our comfortable, middle class "critics" put themselves through the kind of agonized self-criticism I have seen young radicals and young blacks resort to.

Coles: Well, by no means do all radicals question themselves and their assumptions so carefully—and by no means do all middle class "critics" lack a capacity for self-scrutiny and yes, agony. (Some of them are "agonized" if nothing else!) But when you talked about the Weathermen, I thought of Will Campbell and his work with the Klan.

Berrigan: Exactly. I suppose to do so, to reach out to those one may strongly disagree with is to challenge the paramilitary view of man as either conformist or else traitorous. I think we must continually break through the various barriers which forbid us access to our brothers—those who are potentially at least our brothers, and in whose life and death, love it or not, hate it or not, we are involved. One must resist at all costs those rigid dualisms: all good, all bad. Christ saw us as redeemable—and how often he turned his heart to social outcasts! Christ saw us as both more and less than we appear to be. The rich and powerful man can be a hypocrite and fraud; the poor and scorned man can be honest and decent. Those who judge others, let alone attack others in the name of various slogans, must have placed upon them the scrutiny of the Christian eye: Cain may be wearing the skin of Abel in order to cause further bloodshed in the world.

Then there are those who want to change history one way or another. Some of the Marxists I spoke to in Moscow had a strong and almost bitter sense of themselves as the first "new men." I've heard the same thing put much more quietly, and I thought much more richly, on many occasions by resisters who also saw themselves as "new men."

The emergence of a Christian community in any era is mysterious. But we are not in total darkness; the mysterious can also become known to us. Today many heroic people have grown and demonstrated new resources in the face of what we might call the near basket-case to which man has been reduced by the times—by technology, by power politics, by the cold war.

I love something in the very ancient biblical tradition which I understand is also quite alive in Hinduism and the Moslem faith. It has to do with the idea that the new man gets born under the mysterious circumstances of what the Hebrews called the *anaw*, or if he was lucky enough to find himself in a community, the *anawim*. That very rich conception was translated historically in different ways, depending upon the culture; but it had to do quite generally with the redemptive possibilities which become incarnate in one who is despised and considered worthless by the rich and powerful people of his time. Often the man's life was pressed to the point of extreme anguish—such as we read in, say, the forty-ninth chapter of Isaiah or the twenty-first Psalm. Often he is abandoned, again as in Isaiah when he utters, "My God, my God, why have you forsaken me?"—the words which Christ later took to his lips, evidently at the moment of his agony. But it is instructive that this man, so far as we can trace his spiritual physiognomy, is so repeatedly (in various religious traditions) a human reject, a man who finds himself somewhat like Job: there, left and alone, at the gate of the city, cast out, without recourse—and so one whose final hope became the absurdity of believing beyond belief and hoping beyond hope. Mysteriously a few of these fringe figures from time to time have come together and worked toward the redemption of the majority. It is very strange, very mysterious. I think Israel has never really quite been able to forget that magnificent explosion in its own ancient literature—of Isaiah and Jeremiah; and neither has Christianity, because it seems to me Christ declared so explicitly his own solidarity with that tradition at the hour of His death, the tradition of the outsider, the dissenter, the critic who dares speak the extremely upsetting and painful truth.

Now today one can only hope more and more such individuals will appear and fearlessly talk about the alternatives to the political and military institutions which are imperialist and war making and racist and narrowly nationalistic and which presume to declare their right to establish the perimeters within which life may continue or in which death must occur. I really don't know whether my religious and philosophical way of putting these matters is acceptable in any way to the movement; I have had my doubts about it. But at least if the movement can't deal with the kind of images that mean something to me, the movement still has to deal with the issues those images (I believe) suggest. And in circumstances like these (when I am hunted by the police) I feel especially called to declare the images which inspire me in my effort to find meaning in life—and find what needs to be done by all of us. Perhaps in times like our own we are forced back to just a few great figures—in my case, religious figures. The heroic man has been pulled down in our own times—there are so few models of manhood allowed in this great leveling-off decreed by the state. Yet our lives are so obviously and almost willingly impoverished, especially in the white community these days, for various reasons we could go into. No wonder one looks for heroes who broke the confining bonds of their time, who did not worry about what is "respectable" and what the equivalent in their time of the Gallup Poll would show.

The first generation of Christian communities, the ones which appeared after Christ's death, struggled with all of this, even as we do; in the midst of the worst of times, after all, they had seen a new man appear, unpromising though his origins were. John says, "He cannot be explained." At His deepest He is simply not to be studied biologically, and maybe not psychologically, either. He is born not of the flesh, nor of the will of man, but is of God; and John seems to tell us: you can either understand that, or alas, you can't—period. And we have in the first chapter of the Acts of the Apostles a kind of diary which tells us how the early Christians felt, what they struggled with and for. They deliberately and fervently rejected the powers and principalities of their world, and they held to what was essentially this ordinance, given to the new community by the risen Christ: have faith and wait for an event that you can neither bring to pass nor hope to understand. Whence the mystery of Pentecost—and with regard to that the new power of the Holy Spirit was to be measured by the fervor of the rejection on the part of Christians of the old forms of power, the old carnal and military and subversive forms that had ruled for so long, and which Christ had broken through upon His death. Now that new kind of power (which the early Christians waited for and sought eagerly) renders one powerless, continually powerless in this world—subject to the rulers of this world, subject to their courts, and their prisons and their death. Nevertheless that power leads a Christian to his own kind of victory; and that power generates the passion of a long historical tradition—and that power also represents something which can never quite be overcome, can never quite be done away with, can never quite be entirely stamped out, even by those who cleverly call themselves believers but who retain the old kind of power, as we so often witness.

I don't know what the secular analogies of all this are, but I do have a very strong suspicion that they exist. Perhaps we are at a point when, like the early Christians, we must create communities which themselves become signs of hope, signs that the Holy Spirit is indeed coming upon us. Perhaps these communities, peace affirming, contemptuous of existing powers, however mighty and self-righteous, will be made up of the most diverse people, whether it be the despised and exploited field hands of the deep South, or whether it be the imprisoned Klansman who is undergoing his sort of rebirth, or whether it be middle America, or whether it be the resisters whom I know best. It seems to me that "new men" may well appear in many places and under many guises, and that to be alive to the signs those men offer is to be alive to the true hope that is before us. I think that there is simply no end to the mystery and the actuality of rebirth that is occurring in our midst. How it all comes together, how men get to assert themselves in the defense of the defenseless throughout the world, how America becomes reborn and stops its bloodletting—well, those are the questions that remain. But I have no doubt that we are moving along.

Coles: You think these things are going to happen.

Berrigan: No, I think they are actually happening.

Coles: You are almost *infinitely* more optimistic than I am.

Berrigan: Well, it seems to me that at certain points tonight (as I read you) you have been saying the same thing.

Coles: No. I have said that many things are *possible.* I think that you and I have differed all along. You have hope because you believe a significant number of desirable things are happening. I have hope because I have seen a *few* desirable things happen, and I don't think that there is anything in man's nature or mind that necessarily prevents these things from happening. But I do not see widespread possibilities becoming actualities.

Berrigan: Well, I never used that word "widespread." Nor would I. How could I, realistically? I don't think that the kind of rebirth I am talking about ever becomes all that widespread. It seems to me that we are talking about, oh, the hopes of powerless people, but we are also talking about what those hopes may lead to, may generate; and I hope we never indulge ourselves in what might be called the movement counterpart of the body count, the opinion poll, the survey. How could such things become a numbers game?

Coles: History offers us an example of a particular person, a revolutionary, a dissenter, a man condemned to a most humiliating kind of death under the most ignoble of circumstances— who nevertheless emerged as God. The numbers game there was *one* versus *everyone*. Christ was one person, and he wasn't exactly a rich and powerful person; He didn't have atomic bombs at His disposal, nor did He live in the White House or the Kremlin. One is haunted because He certainly did change history, make a new history. God chose Him, obscure though He was, and He set an example for us to follow. On the other hand, just look at what goes on in His name: the desecration— the insulting and awful things that go on in His name. That is the mystery: Christ has inspired us, shown us what a victory He alone could win—but also shown us how a struggle can be lost, can be tarnished and worse. Every day Christ is betrayed by institutions which bear His name, let alone those avowedly uninterested in His life and teachings.

Berrigan: It seems to me that a figure like Bernanos's curé took for granted human malice and suffering and violence and spite; and yet, especially toward the end there, toward his death, he knew that even if everything did not measure up to his hopes, still those hopes were grounded in something inviolable, something that lives on and on, because it is God-inspired. Undoubtedly we are talking here about a "something," a kind of hope, which is hard to describe. To the majority of good people, especially it seems to me in the movement, the sum of the facts before us add up to whatever hope there is. But that is not what I am talking about.

Coles: What *are* you talking about? As you just spoke I felt you trying to say that those pragmatists, those fact-minded people, those practical men who lived in the first century A.D. must to this day—wherever they are—be scratching their heads in confusion.

Berrigan: I am trying to visualize a hope which is based not upon the particular "balance" of good and evil to be found in any given era, but which expresses itself in certain interventions, certain signs, certain hints, certain deeds—all of which press upon us with the breath of the spirit, with the breath of the transcendent. And this being acceptable or not, to most people, I do believe everyone, in one way or another, tries to find some evidence for himself that we are headed for a better world than we now have. Yet, even if right now America were more nearly (not nominally, but in practice) a Christian nation, and even if decency were a public resource, available to our leaders in large amounts, and even if our transgressions had been atoned for—even so I would still be forbidden by my faith to place my primary hope on those (political, social) facts, because I would have to face even such an optimal human situation with a deep understanding that changed programs and policies in and of themselves are a means to something, not ends in themselves. We aim for an ethical community under God—knowing that no particular sign of progress in that direction ought to give us cause to rest, just as no evidence that we are for a while stuck in mud ought to cause us to give up, to lose hope.

Coles: Perhaps some people in what is loosely called "the movement" began in the midsixties to talk among themselves as you have just done. Many youthful activists I knew (in the South, in Appalachia) eventually began to stop concentrating all their efforts on winning over this political leader, or gaining such and such from that political convention. It is not that they became uninterested in politics, or unaware of what they had to do in the political arena. No, they didn't turn "soft" or "naïve" (as those tough-minded "realists" are wont to call *powerful* men like Christ or Gandhi). I think many of them began to see that their struggle was, if they would not call it spiritual, at least profoundly ethical, and could not allow itself to become the property, say, of a particular President of the United States, or of the Democratic Party, meeting in its 1964 or 1968 or 1972 convention.

I am talking about men and women who were in the civil rights movement, young people who were in CORE and SNCC

in 1962 and 1963 and 1964. Some of them are still struggling in
certain communities in this country, in the South and in the
North; and as one gets to know them—as I have gotten to know
them for a decade—one sees that their lives simply cannot be
comprehended in the usual ways we describe lives. I tried in
1964 to talk to my colleagues about the "weariness" that social
struggle causes in participants—and the stubborn determination they also demonstrate, against seemingly impossible odds.
I used then and have continued to summon as best I can a whole
range of language—psychiatric language, psychoanalytic language, sociological language. None of my words and formulations really do justice to what happens over the years to those
young men and women—to their achievements, their failures,
their struggles. This I know, though: they have stayed the course,
and the course I'm talking about here is not a particular political struggle. Their lives have been committed to what I keep
on calling ethical concern. They have waged (bitterly at times
and at other times with gentleness and extraordinary patience)
a consistent struggle with the world around them—a struggle
not unlike, I think, the struggle of the curé in *The Diary of a
Country Priest*. They have been disappointed. They have found
in themselves pride—and sometimes that pride has been un-
masked, sometimes it has gone unnoticed. They have won victories. They have lost many battles. Still, it's been ten years now.
Some of them started this effort when they were twenty, and so
are now thirty. Some started older and so are nearing forty. Now,
no one is giving them congressional medals of honor. No one is
calling them to the White House and patting them on the back.
No politician is calling them heroes, nor do we see them on television screens any more. We may have spotted them on those
screens a few years ago, at particular demonstrations in the
South or for that matter the North. But no more; they are really
out of sight now. Yet, they persist. They do their work. They stay
away from reporters and cameras—and social scientists. They
have learned to be suspicious of political "compromises" or "set-
tlements" or gestures of solidarity from high officials. They get

up and work and become tired and go to sleep. They are in a way living the hard, tough, bleak yet compelling and often quietly dramatic lives Faulkner showed to be the lot of white yeomen or black sharecroppers in the South.

I guess one calls such a struggle a spiritual one; I don't know quite how to define the word "spiritual"—maybe that's your territory or maybe I shouldn't be saying that, because I do feel we all have an obligation to achieve whatever spiritual direction we can in whatever places we can locate. But who can say he's found that direction, a spiritual direction, for himself or in others? Well, perhaps we can speak about others—but never about ourselves. Once I heard Lyndon Johnson exhort us to "stay the course." I think he had Vietnam in mind. Well, those young men (in obscure towns in Georgia or Mississippi, in obscure tenements in various cities of this country, up in the hills of Appalachia) have all stayed the course. They are Americans. And they are silent Americans for the most part; that is, we don't hear from them very much. But they are going along, doing their work; and I suspect they may be "new men" and "new women."

Berrigan: What you describe reminds me of some Vietnamese I have met; they have patience and the power of endurance and one must almost call it a revolutionary virtue, a revolutionary sense of history. They know the long haul ahead. They are not noisy or demanding or eager to prove immediately successful. I think some of us in the movement have a lot to learn from them.

Coles: I would most emphatically agree with that. Perhaps it is harder in America to be quiet and self-effacing and patient. So, it is all the more remarkable that at least some black and white workers in various parts of this country had indeed shunned histrionics, and avoided rancor and deviousness and calculated vulgarity and thoughtlessness. This sense of history that you mention seeing among so many Vietnamese—many of these young activists have had to work hard for such a perspective. I think Americans are a vigorous, immediate people, concerned with the present more than either the past or the future. Maybe that is why I found it almost unnerving to talk with young people in an obscure part of Appalachia or the South or on the street of a ghetto and hear them mention the *limited* things they are attempting. I guess I was brought up to believe that in this country nothing is limited; we can do what we want—and fast. Instead I have heard young Americans mention that others have preceded them, others will follow, and their particular task is simply to do all they can while they can. They disclaim "goals"; they have no Five Year Plans, no Ten Year Plans. They don't want a New Deal or a Fair Deal or a New Freedom. They laugh at slogans, and they feel they find freedom in their work. They also find freedom by refusing to look upon their struggle as tied to a particular period of time. It's no easy thing to think like that, and one can't all the time. If one is lucky one gains such a perspective, then loses it, then gains it back.

Berrigan: Much of this discussion with you emphasizes, I now realize, what I suppose could be called a spirit of "Christian tentativeness" in the face of the exhausting and the consuming facts of human upheaval. I could put it perhaps very clumsily by saying that man is forbidden to set up false gods, but he is invited to have his heroes. We must avoid taking ourselves so seriously that we march brusquely through any impasse, convinced that we are right, we have the answer—we are gods. A man like Gandhi possessed a kind of humility which forbade him the pursuit of personal status; he never wanted to be a Caesar.

Coles: But yet he had to struggle with arrogance and pride, even as we all do.

Berrigan: Am I mistaken that toward the end of his life he simply said in his diary that he had yet to perform one perfect nonviolent action—he wrote so after a lifetime of discipline and of struggle. I thought that was a marvelous self-revelation.

Coles: I like your term "Christian tentativeness." I wish we saw in this world more Christian tentativeness and Christian passion. Obviously we need a mixture of the two, because Christian tentativeness can, like anything, become weak and vague. But a mixture of passion and tentativeness strikes some bell in me about people whom I admire: they are not dogmatic and histrionic and self-serving, even as they are tempted to be; they somehow struggle through, muddle through, tentatively yet with passion—and with a clear sense of what they believe in, even as they struggle from time to time about how to achieve what they want for this world.

Berrigan: What does all this have to do (especially in regard to these young people whom you have been describing) with their attitude toward death? I very much want to understand how the young people you mention live as they do. I think in order to live as they do one must have come face to face with the fact of death, its hovering presence and proximity. I can't conceive that such people are subject to any ruling fears.

Coles: They do indeed have fears, but in that regard their struggle is not unlike Christ's. They know that death faces them, even as He did. They believe that there is life to be fought for, and that insofar as they are afraid of death, they are human. Like Christ on the Cross they know doubt and despair, and yet trust in Someone, Something, larger than themselves. I believe they are struggling on a frontier larger than any particular social struggle can define. They are struggling for life and in that sense you are right: they must indeed come to terms with death, because death in all its implications is what they are fighting—exploitation, brutality, racism, colonialism, and on and on. Stephen Spender said it well: they are "those who in their lives fought for life." Spender says they are "truly great," and they are great because they are struggling for the lives of people who are denied life by existing ideologies and institutions. And in struggling for life one has to fear death, has to face one's own vulnerability—which can lead to a kind of living death, and by that I mean the death of those who become smug and self-important and cleverly mean or merely indifferent. And then there is the living death so many of us know: we have no idea what we really want—beyond the next purchase or rung of the ladder; we don't have any idea what to struggle for. Maybe we're a lot worse off than these young and apparently desperate youths, working "out there" against such high odds.

Berrigan: Paul says somewhere in one of his letters something very simple about himself. Speaking of that rocky course he was on (which included floggings and imprisonment and exile and all the rest) he says: "I die daily." I think that is a wonderfully brief and striking description of the kind of constant rebirth that is required of all of us. And if we are to be born again, we must be prepared to suffer and die.

Afterword

by Daniel Berrigan

"The Geography of Faith" was first mapped out, thanks to the hospitality of Bob and Jane Coles, more than three decades ago.

The more things change, as the French say caustically, the more they remain the same.

In the years since then, the Vietnam adventuring has hardly been succeeded by secular canniness or wisdom ("Let's admit it, we got badly burned on that one—never again!").

We have heard no such admission, even in private, much less in practice. Since 1971, one could assemble a roster of incursions, invasions, subversions, interferences, arms deals, covert "actions," air strikes, sanctions, depleted uranium land, and air wars. Since 1971, Americans have bombed eighteen countries. In not one of these targets has a government arisen respectful of human or civil rights.

Dr. Coles might be tempted to diagnose this cosmic rage as a kind of collective psychosis, an obsessive method laid on madness. The "reasoning" of presidents and pentagonal nabobs goes, one ventures, something like this, a formula contrived in a national madhouse: "If a tactic utterly fails, redouble it."

In those weeks, we spread out the map of the world, the world as it was then, or as we saw it then (and pardon our language, a sign of the times, innocently sexist). A world of "families," of "pride and violence," of some of us "at the edge" (and how long that edgy existence was to perdure!), of "compassionate men *[sic]* and political men *[sic]*," and so on.

What we never imagined—how could we—was how that world would look some thirty years later.

It was a mercy, that ignorance, that veil drawn across the future.

As to the text of the "Geography" herewith mapped once more, it seems to me that it holds accurate today.

In the quarter century since the Coles family welcomed me into their home, the landscape of faith has been tested by fire, repeatedly. What we now know, and even now and again rejoice to know, is that the terrain of faith remains intact, though wounded.

The map has been hardly dealt with; faith has been, so to speak, bombed, invaded, covertly and openly tempted to assimilate to a culture of death.

Despite all, I venture that the geography of thirty years ago is still discernable. Anchored in the world, even so terrifying a world, faith perdures, faith works.

Faith also celebrates. I append two poems; the first is dedicated to my brother Philip and my brother Jesuit, Steven Kelly, and to Susan Crane. We mourn and rejoice; at this writing our noble friends are prisoners of conscience.

The second poem celebrates an event of this past Holy Week in New York City. A number of us were arrested at a vast war museum docked in the Hudson River. There, multitudes of school children are inducted each day into war and violence. We objected, consequentially.

(April 22, 2001, commemoration of Kathe Kollwitz, Artist)

Advent, 1999
Those I Love Are Subjected
Once More to a Farcical Trial

Reverberations, motions of spirit—
        only monks or mystics are attentive.

    Beneath the commotions of violated justice,
        the rancor of death's-head judges—

        go deep, deeper.

    Soul stirs like the faint flutter
        of Lazarus' fingers' start
to lift the gauzy shroud from face.
      (Caravaggio, that volatile genius, but
        Christ thought of it first).

     Lazarus longs to breathe. He clutches thin air
though a moment ago, thought of breath
      slept forever,

        dead bones
    stacked back to back, all odds
      against life.

    Now face to face.

And ourselves stirred, who a moment past
    dared not summon

—shall we risk it?—the Real Thing.

The Friday We Name Good
(2001; At the SS Intrepid War Museum, 8 friends were arrested)

It seemed plain as uncut bread
which nonetheless is cut at need

(a loaf, truth for the mind's palate)—

countering sound sense; "No bread, but My Body."
and this; "Given for you."

We sought the bread of truth
in hell's kitchen, the New York "Tombs"
on Good Friday, while Jesus atremble, died;

down down He went, a plummet, as though
cross were a craft, to Shoel.
                              We ate fire,
no bread in the stoked iron oven
of no truth.

                    But ours.

Angels bearing bread, entered
like dawn, the bolts and bars
sundered.
              We broke and passed the loaf.

Portions fell like manna
on prisoners;
                    "What you doin' here?"

We knew, yes. "My Body, given for you."

Have some.
It was good.

Glossary of Terms, Movements, and Names

Bernanos, Georges (1888–1948): French novelist and political thinker whose influential novel, *Diary of a Country Priest,* chronicles the life of a village priest whose congregation cares little for the Church. The book was foundational in the spiritual thought of Thomas Merton, Dorothy Day, and Simone Weil, among many others.

Berrigan, Philip (1923–): Daniel Berrigan's brother and partner in the antiwar protest movement. Like his brother, Philip was ordained a Catholic priest, but he left the priesthood in the 1960s to marry a fellow activist, Sr. Elizabeth McAlister. Imprisoned many times in his career, he remains active to this day in the movement for nuclear disarmament.

Black Panther Party (often referred to by Daniel Berrigan as simply "the Panthers"): A Black separatist wing that grew out of the civil rights movement. Founded in 1966 by Huey P. Newton and Bobby Seale, the Panthers generally disagreed with the pacifist tactics espoused by Martin Luther King, Jr., and the rest of the peace and civil rights movements.

Bonhoeffer, Dietrich (1906–1945): German Lutheran pastor and theologian who strongly opposed Hitler and the Nazis, for which he was imprisoned and executed.

Carmichael, Stokely (1941–1998): Prominent in the organization of the SNCC, he later urged African Americans to reject American societal values and to form their own separatist organizations. He eventually joined the Black Panther Party as their "honorary prime minister." He is famous for coining the slogans "Black Power" and "Black is beautiful."

Catholic Worker Movement: Movement founded in 1933 by Roman Catholic social activists Dorothy Day and Peter Maurin. It is best known for its houses of hospitality, found in many American inner city neighborhoods, which exist to feed and clothe the poor and the homeless, as well as for its newspaper, *The Catholic Worker* (newsstand price 1 cent). Catholic Worker communities are also known for activity in support of labor unions, human rights, cooperatives, and the development of a nonviolent culture.

Catonsville Nine: A group of people, including Daniel Berrigan, who, as a protest against the Vietnam War, destroyed the draft records in the court of Catonsville, Maryland, a suburb of Baltimore.

Chavez, Cesar (1927–1993): Mexican-American labor leader, founder of the United Farm Workers Organizing Committee, and inspirational activist whose ideas and tactics are studied by today's labor leaders. In 1968 he organized a famous boycott of California table grapes in a drive to achieve a labor contract for farm workers.

CORE: Congress of Racial Equality. A New York–based civil rights organization that, with the SNCC, organized the 1961 "Freedom Rides," in which a number of anti-segregation activists rode buses from Washington, D.C., challenging segregationist policies throughout the South.

Eberhardt, David: One of the "Catonsville Nine," who, with Daniel Berrigan, destroyed draft records in Catonsville, Maryland.

Marcuse, Herbert (1898–1979): French philosopher, social theorist, and political activist, celebrated in the media as "Father of the New Left." His theory of "one-dimensional" society provided critical perspectives on contemporary capitalist and state communist societies and his notion of "the great refusal" won him renown as a theorist of revolutionary change and "liberation from the affluent society."

Reuther, Rosemary Radford: Catholic feminist theologian and a supporter of Daniel Berrigan and the Catonsville Nine.

Satyagraha (Sanskrit: "truth force"): Mohandas K. Gandhi's principle of nonviolence—that the power of truth, without the use of force or violence, was the most effective means to bring about political and social change. The principle was adopted, famously, by Martin Luther King, Jr., and through him had a profound effect on the American civil rights movement. Many of the leaders of today's protest movements continue to be influenced by the principle, such as those involved in the demonstrations against the World Trade Organization in Seattle in 1999.

Self-immolation: The practice of setting oneself on fire as a form of protest. It was used by Buddhist monks in Vietnam in the 1960s and, more recently, by protesters in Beijing's Tiananmen Square demonstrations.

SNCC: Student Nonviolent Coordinating Committee. A political organization formed in 1960 by Black college students dedicated to overturning segregation in the South, and to giving young Blacks a stronger voice in the civil rights movement. The "sit-in" movement, in which activists challenged segregation in public places, arose from the SNCC, as did the push for universal voter registration in the South in the 1960s.

Spellman, Francis Cardinal (1889–1967): Politically influential Roman Catholic archbishop of New York from 1939 to 1967. An ardent anti-communist, Cardinal Spellman was a key supporter of President Lyndon Johnson's escalation of American involvement in the Vietnam War.

Tillich, Paul (1886–1965): German Protestant theologian who lived in the United States after his expulsion from Germany by the Nazis in 1933. One of his particular concerns was that theology be in constant interaction with the real concerns of the times.

Weathermen: A militant antiwar faction that grew out of the Students for a Democratic Society (SDS) organization in the 1960s. Though the SDS was originally pacifist, the Weathermen faction came to feel that the gravity of the U.S. involvement in the Vietnam War justified their use of terrorist tactics.

Weil, Simone (1909–1943): French philosopher and political activist who underwent a kind of conversion to Christianity, yet rejected baptism, as a witness to abuses of power of the Church's hierarchy. The articulation of her position is found in her book *Waiting for God.*

Notes

Notes

Notes

Notes

Notes

About SKYLIGHT PATHS Publishing

SkyLight Paths Publishing is creating a place where people of different spiritual traditions come together for challenge and inspiration, a place where we can help each other understand the mystery that lies at the heart of our existence.

Through spirituality, our religious beliefs are increasingly becoming a part of our lives—rather than *apart* from our lives. While many of us may be more interested than ever in spiritual growth, we may be less firmly planted in traditional religion. Yet, we do want to deepen our relationship to the sacred, to learn from our own as well as from other faith traditions, and to practice in new ways.

SkyLight Paths sees both believers and seekers as a community that increasingly transcends traditional boundaries of religion and denomination—people wanting to learn from each other, *walking together, finding the way.*

We at SkyLight Paths take great care to produce beautiful books that present meaningful spiritual content in a form that reflects the art of making high quality books. Therefore, we want to acknowledge those who contributed to the production of this book.

PRODUCTION
Tim Holtz & Bridgett Taylor

EDITORIAL
Amanda Dupuis, Martha McKinney,
Polly Short Mahoney & Emily Wichland

COVER DESIGN
Bridgett Taylor

PRINTING AND BINDING
Versa Press, East Peoria, Illinois

Spirituality

Who Is My God?
An Innovative Guide to Finding Your Spiritual Identity
Created by *the Editors at SkyLight Paths*

Spiritual Type™ + Tradition Indicator = Spiritual Identity

Your Spiritual Identity is an undeniable part of who you are—whether you've thought much about it or not. This dynamic resource provides a helpful framework to begin or deepen your spiritual growth. Start by taking the unique Spiritual Identity Self-Test™; tabulate your results; then explore one, two or more of twenty-eight faiths/spiritual paths followed in America today. "An innovative and entertaining way to think—and rethink—about your own spiritual path, or perhaps even to find one." —Dan Wakefield, author of *How Do We Know When It's God?*
6 x 9, 160 pp, Quality PB Original, ISBN 1-893361-08-X **$15.95**

Spiritual Manifestos: *Visions for Renewed Religious Life in America from Young Spiritual Leaders of Many Faiths*
Edited by *Niles Elliot Goldstein*; Preface by *Martin E. Marty*

Discover the reasons why so many people have kept organized religion at arm's length.

Here, ten young spiritual leaders, most in their mid-thirties, representing the spectrum of religious traditions—Protestant, Catholic, Jewish, Buddhist, Unitarian Universalist—present the innovative ways they are transforming our spiritual communities and our lives. "These ten articulate young spiritual leaders engender hope for the vitality of 21st-century religion." —Forrest Church, Minister of All Souls Church in New York City
6 x 9, 256 pp, HC, ISBN 1-893361-09-8 **$21.95**

  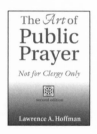 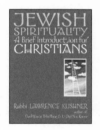

Jewish Spirituality: *A Brief Introduction for Christians*
by *Lawrence Kushner*

Lawrence Kushner, whose award-winning books have brought Jewish spirituality to life for countless readers of all faiths and backgrounds, tailors his unique style to address Christian's questions, revealing the essence of Judaism in a way that people whose own tradition traces its roots to Judaism can understand and enjoy. Offers Christian readers tools to strengthen their own faith. 5½ x 8½, 112 pp, Quality PB Original, ISBN 1-58023-150-0 **$12.95**

The Art of Public Prayer: *Not for Clergy Only,* 2nd Edition
by *Lawrence A. Hoffman*

A resource for worshipers today looking to change hardened worship patterns that stand in the way of everyday spirituality.

Written for laypeople and clergy of any denomination, this ecumenical introduction to meaningful public prayer is for everyone who cares about religion today.
6 x 9, 288 pp, Quality PB, ISBN 1-893361-06-3 **$17.95**

Spirituality

Inspired Lives: *Exploring the Role of Faith and Spirituality in the Lives of Extraordinary People*

by *Joanna Laufer* & *Kenneth S. Lewis*

Contributors include *Ang Lee, Wynton Marsalis, Kathleen Norris,* and many more

How faith transforms the lives and work of the creative and innovative people in our world.

In this moving book, soul-searching conversations unearth the importance of spirituality and personal faith for more than forty artists and innovators who have made a real difference in our world through their work. 6 x 9, 256 pp, Quality PB, ISBN 1-893361-33-0 **$16.95**

Women Pray
Voices through the Ages, from Many Faiths, Cultures, and Traditions

Edited and with introductions by *Monica Furlong*

Many ways—new and old—to communicate with the Divine.

This beautiful gift book celebrates the rich variety of ways women around the world have called out to the Divine—with words of joy, praise, gratitude, wonder, petition, longing, and even anger—from the ancient world up to our own time. Prayers from women of nearly every religious or spiritual background give us an eloquent expression of what it means to communicate with God. 5 x 7¼, 256 pp, Deluxe HC with ribbon marker, ISBN 1-893361-25-X **$19.95**

Zen Effects: *The Life of Alan Watts*

by *Monica Furlong*

The first and only full-length biography of one of the most charismatic spiritual leaders of the twentieth century—now back in print!

Through his widely popular books and lectures, Alan Watts (1915–1973) did more to introduce Eastern philosophy and religion to Western minds than any figure before or since. Here is the only biography of this charismatic figure, who served as Zen teacher, Anglican priest, lecturer, academic, entertainer, a leader of the San Francisco renaissance, and author of more than 30 books, including *The Way of Zen, Psychotherapy East and West* and *The Spirit of Zen.* 6 x 9, 264 pp, Quality PB, ISBN 1-893361-32-2 **$16.95**

Simone Weil: *A Modern Pilgrimage*

by *Robert Coles*

The extraordinary life of the spiritual philosopher who's been called both saint and madwoman.

The French writer and philosopher Simone Weil (1906–1943) devoted her life to a search for God—while avoiding membership in organized religion. Robert Coles' intriguing study of Weil details her short, eventful life, and is an insightful portrait of the beloved and controversial thinker whose life and writings influenced many (from T.S. Eliot to Adrienne Rich to Albert Camus), and continue to inspire seekers everywhere. 6 x 9, 208 pp, Quality PB, ISBN 1-893361-34-9 **$16.95**

Spirituality

Three Gates to Meditation Practice
A Personal Journey into Sufism, Buddhism, and Judaism
by *David A. Cooper*

Shows us how practicing within more than one spiritual tradition can lead us to our true home.

Here are over fifteen years from the journey of "post-denominational rabbi" David A. Cooper, author of *God Is a Verb*, and his wife, Shoshana—years in which the Coopers explored a rich variety of practices, from chanting Sufi *dhikr* to Buddhist Vipassanā meditation, to the study of kabbalah and esoteric Judaism. Their experience demonstrates that the spiritual path is really completely within our reach, whoever we are, whatever we do—as long as we are willing to practice it. 5½ x 8½, 240 pp, Quality PB, ISBN 1-893361-22-5 **$16.95**

Praying with Our Hands: *Twenty-One Practices of Embodied Prayer from the World's Spiritual Traditions*
by *Jon M. Sweeney;* Photographs by *Jennifer J. Wilson;*
Foreword by *Mother Tessa Bielecki;* Afterword by *Taitetsu Unno, Ph.D.*

A spiritual guidebook for bringing prayer into our bodies.

What gives our prayers meaning? How can we carry a prayerful spirit throughout our everyday lives? This inspiring book of reflections and accompanying photographs shows us twenty-one simple ways of using our hands to speak to God, to enrich our devotion and ritual. All express the various approaches of the world's religious traditions to bringing the body into worship. Spiritual traditions represented include Anglican, Sufi, Zen, Roman Catholic, Yoga, Shaker, Hindu, Jewish, Pentecostal, Eastern Orthodox, and many others.
8 x 8, 96 pp, 22 duotone photographs, Quality PB Original, ISBN 1-893361-16-0 **$16.95**

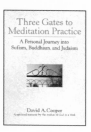  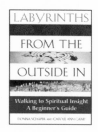

Labyrinths from the Outside In
Walking to Spiritual Insight—a Beginner's Guide
by *Donna Schaper* & *Carole Ann Camp*

The user-friendly, interfaith guide to making and using labyrinths— for meditation, prayer, and celebration.

Labyrinth walking is a spiritual exercise *anyone* can do. And it's rare among such practices in that it can be done by people together, regardless of their religious backgrounds or lack thereof. This accessible guide unlocks the mysteries of the labyrinth for all of us, providing ideas for using the labyrinth walk for prayer, meditation, and celebrations to mark the most important moments in life. Includes instructions for making a labyrinth of your own and finding one in your area.
6 x 9, 208 pp, b/w illus. and photographs, Quality PB Original, ISBN 1-893361-18-7 **$16.95**

Spirituality

One God Clapping: *The Spiritual Path of a Zen Rabbi*

by *Alan Lew* with *Sherril Jaffe* **AWARD WINNER!**

Firsthand account of a spiritual journey from Zen Buddhist practitioner to rabbi.

A fascinating personal story of a Jewish meditation expert's roundabout spiritual journey from Zen Buddhist practitioner to rabbi. An insightful source of inspiration for each of us who is on the journey to find God in today's multi-faceted spiritual world.
5½ x 8½, 336 pp, Quality PB, ISBN 1-58023-115-2 **$16.95**

The Way of a Pilgrim: *Annotated & Explained*

Translation & annotation by *Gleb Pokrovsky;*

Foreword by *Andrew Harvey*, SkyLight Illuminations series editor

The classic of Russian spirituality—now with facing-page commentary that illuminates and explains the text.

This delightful account is the story of one man who sets out to learn the prayer of the heart—also known as the "Jesus prayer"—and how the practice transforms his existence. This SkyLight Illuminations edition guides you through an abridged version of the text with facing-page annotations explaining the names, terms and references.
5½ x 8½, 160 pp, Quality PB, ISBN 1-893361-31-4 **$14.95**

The Way Into Jewish Mystical Tradition

by *Lawrence Kushner*

Explains the principles of Jewish mystical thinking, their religious and spiritual significance, and how they relate to our lives. A book that allows us to experience and understand the Jewish mystical approach to our place in the world. 6 x 9, 224 pp, HC, ISBN 1-58023-029-6 **$21.95**

The New Millennium Spiritual Journey
Change Your Life—Develop Your Spiritual Priorities with Help from Today's Most Inspiring Spiritual Teachers

Created by *the Editors at SkyLight Paths*

A life-changing resource for reimagining your spiritual life.

Set your own course of reflection and spiritual transformation with the help of self-tests, spirituality exercises, sacred texts from many traditions, time capsule pages, and helpful suggestions from more than 20 spiritual teachers, including Karen Armstrong, Sylvia Boorstein and Dr. Andrew Weil. 7 x 9, 144 pp, Quality PB Original, ISBN 1-893361-05-5 **$16.95**

Spirituality

Honey from the Rock
An Introduction to Jewish Mysticism
by *Lawrence Kushner*

An insightful and absorbing introduction to the ten gates of Jewish mysticism and how it applies to daily life. "The easiest introduction to Jewish mysticism you can read."
6 x 9, 176 pp, Quality PB, ISBN 1-58023-073-3 **$15.95**

Eyes Remade for Wonder
The Way of Jewish Mysticism and Sacred Living
A Lawrence Kushner Reader

Intro. by *Thomas Moore*, author of *Care of the Soul*

Whether you are new to Kushner or a devoted fan, you'll find inspiration here. With samplings from each of Kushner's works, and a generous amount of new material, this book is to be read and reread, each time discovering deeper layers of meaning in our lives.
6 x 9, 240 pp, Quality PB, ISBN 1-58023-042-3 **$16.95**; HC, ISBN 1-58023-014-8 **$23.95**

Invisible Lines of Connection
Sacred Stories of the Ordinary
by *Lawrence Kushner* AWARD WINNER!

Through his everyday encounters with family, friends, colleagues and strangers, Kushner takes us deeply into our lives, finding flashes of spiritual insight in the process.
5½ x 8½, 160 pp, Quality PB, ISBN 1-879045-98-2 **$15.95**; HC, ISBN 1-879045-52-4 **$21.95**

  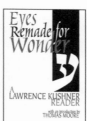  

Finding Joy
A Practical Spiritual Guide to Happiness
by *Dannel I. Schwartz* with *Mark Hass* AWARD WINNER!

Explains how to find joy through a time honored, creative—and surprisingly practical—approach based on the teachings of Jewish mysticism and Kabbalah.
6 x 9, 192 pp, Quality PB, ISBN 1-58023-009-1 **$14.95**; HC, ISBN 1-879045-53-2 **$19.95**

Ancient Secrets
Using the Stories of the Bible to Improve Our Everyday Lives
by *Rabbi Levi Meier, Ph.D.* AWARD WINNER!

Drawing on a broad range of wisdom writings, distinguished rabbi and psychologist Levi Meier takes a thoughtful, wise and fresh approach to showing us how to apply the stories of the Bible to our everyday lives.
5½ x 8½, 288 pp, Quality PB, ISBN 1-58023-064-4 **$16.95**

Spirituality

A Heart of Stillness
A Complete Guide to Learning the Art of Meditation
by *David A. Cooper*

The only complete, nonsectarian guide to meditation, from one of our most respected spiritual teachers.

Experience what mystics have experienced for thousands of years. *A Heart of Stillness* helps you acquire on your own, with minimal guidance, the skills of various styles of meditation. Draws upon the wisdom teachings of Christianity, Judaism, Buddhism, Hinduism, and Islam as it teaches you the processes of purification, concentration, and mastery in detail.
5½ x 8½, 272 pp, Quality PB, ISBN 1-893361-03-9 **$16.95**

Silence, Simplicity & Solitude
A Complete Guide to Spiritual Retreat at Home
by *David A. Cooper*

The classic personal spiritual retreat guide that enables readers to create their own self-guided spiritual retreat at home.

Award-winning author David Cooper traces personal mystical retreat in all of the world's major traditions, describing the varieties of spiritual practices for modern spiritual seekers. Cooper shares the techniques and practices that encompass the personal spiritual retreat experience, allowing readers to enhance their meditation practices and create an effective, self-guided spiritual retreat in their own homes—without the instruction of a meditation teacher. 5½ x 8½, 336 pp, Quality PB, ISBN 1-893361-04-7 **$16.95**

  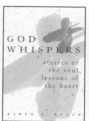  

God Whispers: *Stories of the Soul, Lessons of the Heart*
by Rabbi Karyn D. Kedar 6 x 9, 176 pp, Quality PB, ISBN 1-58023-088-1 **$15.95**

The Empty Chair: *Finding Hope and Joy—*
Timeless Wisdom from a Hasidic Master, Rebbe Nachman of Breslov **AWARD WINNER!**
Adapted by Moshe Mykoff and the Breslov Research Institute
4 x 6, 128 pp, Deluxe PB, 2-color text, ISBN 1-879045-67-2 **$9.95**

The Gentle Weapon: *Prayers for Everyday and Not-So-Everyday Moments*
Adapted from the Wisdom of Rebbe Nachman of Breslov by Moshe Mykoff and
S. C. Mizrahi, with the Breslov Research Institute
4 x 6, 144 pp, Deluxe PB, 2-color text, ISBN 1-58023-022-9 **$9.95**

Children's Spirituality

Becoming Me: *A Story of Creation*

by *Martin Boroson*

For ages 4 & up

Full-color illus. by *Christopher Gilvan-Cartwright*

Told in the personal "voice" of the Creator, here is a story about creation and relationship that is about each one of us. In simple words and with radiant illustrations, the Creator tells an intimate story about love, about friendship and playing, about our world—and about ourselves. And with each turn of the page, we're reminded that we just might be closer to our Creator than we think!

8 x 10, 32 pp, Full-color illus., HC, ISBN 1-893361-11-X **$16.95**

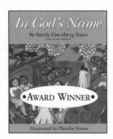

A Prayer for the Earth

The Story of Naamah, Noah's Wife
by *Sandy Eisenberg Sasso*
Full-color illus. by *Bethanne Andersen*

For ages 4 & up

This new story, based on an ancient text, opens readers' religious imaginations to new ideas about the well-known story of the Flood. When God tells Noah to bring the animals of the world onto the ark, God also calls on Naamah, Noah's wife, to save each plant on Earth. "A lovely tale. . . . Children of all ages should be drawn to this parable for our times." —Tomie de Paola, artist/author of books for children

9 x 12, 32 pp, HC, Full-color illus., ISBN 1-879045-60-5 **$16.95**

In God's Name

For ages 4 & up

by *Sandy Eisenberg Sasso*; Full-color illus. by *Phoebe Stone*

Like an ancient myth in its poetic text and vibrant illustrations, this award-winning modern fable about the search for God's name celebrates the diversity and, at the same time, the unity of all the people of the world.

9 x 12, 32 pp, HC, Full-color illus., ISBN 1-879045-26-5 **$16.95**

The 11th Commandment

For all ages

Wisdom from Our Children
by *The Children of America*

"If there were an Eleventh Commandment, what would it be?" Children of many religious denominations across America answer this question—in their own drawings and words. "A rare book of spiritual celebration for all people, of all ages, for all time." —*Bookviews*

8 x 10, 48 pp, HC, Full-color illus., ISBN 1-879045-46-X **$16.95**

Children's Spirituality

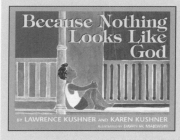

Because Nothing Looks Like God
by *Lawrence and Karen Kushner*
Full-color illus. by *Dawn W. Majewski*

For ages 4 & up

MULTICULTURAL, NONDENOMINATIONAL, NONSECTARIAN

Real-life examples of happiness and sadness—from goodnight stories, to the hope and fear felt the first time at bat, to the closing moments of life—introduce children to the possibilities of spiritual life. A vibrant way for children—and their adults—to explore what, where, and how God is in our lives.
11 x 8½, 32 pp, HC, Full-color illus., ISBN 1-58023-092-X **$16.95**

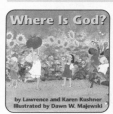

Where Is God? (A Board Book)

For ages 0–4

by *Lawrence and Karen Kushner*; Full-color illus. by *Dawn W. Majewski*

A gentle way for young children to explore how God is with us every day, in every way. Abridged from *Because Nothing Looks Like God* by Lawrence and Karen Kushner and specially adapted to board book format to delight and inspire young readers.
5 x 5, 24 pp, Board, Full-color illus., ISBN 1-893361-17-9 **$7.95**

What Does God Look Like? (A Board Book)

For ages 0–4

by *Lawrence and Karen Kushner*; Full-color illus. by *Dawn W. Majewski*

A simple way for young children to explore the ways that we "see" God. Abridged from *Because Nothing Looks Like God* by Lawrence and Karen Kushner and specially adapted to board book format to delight and inspire young readers.
5 x 5, 24 pp, Board, Full-color illus., ISBN 1-893361-23-3 **$7.95**

How Does God Make Things Happen? (A Board Book)

For ages 0–4

by *Lawrence and Karen Kushner*; Full-color illus. by *Dawn W. Majewski*

A charming invitation for young children to explore how God makes things happen in our world. Abridged from *Because Nothing Looks Like God* by Lawrence and Karen Kushner and specially adapted to board book format to delight and inspire young readers.
5 x 5, 24 pp, Board, Full-color illus., ISBN 1-893361-24-1 **$7.95**

What Is God's Name? (A Board Book)

For ages 0–4

by *Sandy Eisenberg Sasso*; Full-color illus. by *Phoebe Stone*

Everyone and everything in the world has a name. What is God's name? Abridged from the award-winning *In God's Name* by Sandy Eisenberg Sasso and specially adapted to board book format to delight and inspire young readers.
5 x 5, 24 pp, Board, Full-color illus., ISBN 1-893361-10-1 **$7.95**

Children's Spirituality

In Our Image
God's First Creatures
by *Nancy Sohn Swartz*
Full-color illus. by *Melanie Hall*

For ages 4 & up

A playful new twist on the Creation story—from the perspective of the animals. Celebrates the interconnectedness of nature and the harmony of all living things. "The vibrantly colored illustrations nearly leap off the page in this delightful interpretation." —*School Library Journal*

"A message all children should hear, presented in words and pictures that children will find irresistible." —*Rabbi Harold Kushner*, author of *When Bad Things Happen to Good People*

9 x 12, 32 pp, HC, Full-color illus., ISBN 1-879045-99-0 **$16.95**

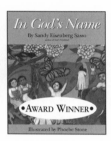

God's Paintbrush

For ages 4 & up

by *Sandy Eisenberg Sasso*; Full-color illus. by *Annette Compton*

Invites children of all faiths and backgrounds to encounter God openly in their own lives. Wonderfully interactive; provides questions adult and child can explore together at the end of each episode. "An excellent way to honor the imaginative breadth and depth of the spiritual life of the young." —Dr. Robert Coles, Harvard University
11 x 8½, 32 pp, HC, Full-color illus., ISBN 1-879045-22-2 **$16.95**

Also available: **A Teacher's Guide**
8½ x 11, 32 pp, PB, ISBN 1-879045-57-5 **$8.95**

God's Paintbrush Celebration Kit 9½ x 12, HC, Includes 5 sessions/40 full-color Activity Sheets and Teacher Folder with complete instructions, ISBN 1-58023-050-4 **$21.95**

In God's Name

For ages 4 & up

by *Sandy Eisenberg Sasso*; Full-color illus. by *Phoebe Stone*

Like an ancient myth in its poetic text and vibrant illustrations, this award-winning modern fable about the search for God's name celebrates the diversity and, at the same time, the unity of all the people of the world. "What a lovely, healing book!" —Madeleine L'Engle
9 x 12, 32 pp, HC, Full-color illus., ISBN 1-879045-26-5 **$16.95**

Other Interesting Books—Spirituality

How to Be a Perfect Stranger, In 2 Volumes
A Guide to Etiquette in Other People's Religious Ceremonies
Ed. by *Stuart M. Matlins* & *Arthur J. Magida* **AWARD WINNERS!**

Explains the rituals and celebrations of North America's major religions/denominations, helping an interested guest to feel comfortable, participate to the fullest extent possible, and avoid violating anyone's religious principles. Answers practical questions from the perspective of *any* other faith.

Vol. 1: North America's Largest Faiths
VOL. 1 COVERS: Assemblies of God • Baptist • Buddhist • Christian Church (Disciples of Christ) • Christian Science • Churches of Christ • Episcopalian/Anglican • Greek Orthodox • Hindu • Islam • Jehovah's Witnesses • Jewish • Lutheran • Methodist • Mormon • Presbyterian • Quaker • Roman Catholic • Seventh-day Adventist • United Church of Canada • United Church of Christ 6 x 9, 432 pp, Quality PB, ISBN 1-893361-01-2 **$19.95**

Vol. 2: More Faiths in North America
VOL. 2 COVERS: African American Methodist Churches • Baha'i • Christian and Missionary Alliance • Christian Congregation • Church of the Brethren • Church of the Nazarene • Evangelical Free Church • International Church of the Foursquare Gospel • International Pentecostal Holiness Church • Mennonite/Amish • Native American/First Nations • Orthodox Churches • Pentecostal Church of God • Reformed Church • Sikh • Unitarian Universalist • Wesleyan 6 x 9, 416 pp, Quality PB, ISBN 1-893361-02-0 **$19.95**

  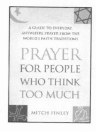

Prayer for People Who Think Too Much
A Guide to Everyday, Anywhere Prayer from the World's Faith Traditions
by *Mitch Finley*

Helps us make prayer a natural part of daily living.
Takes a thoughtful look at how each major faith tradition incorporates prayer into *daily* life. Explores Christian sacraments, Jewish holy days, Muslim daily prayer, "mindfulness" in Buddhism, and more, to help you better understand and enhance your own prayer practices. "I love this book." —Caroline Myss, author of *Anatomy of the Spirit*
5½ x 8½, 224 pp, Quality PB, ISBN 1-893361-21-7 **$16.95**; HC, ISBN 1-893361-00-4 **$21.95**

Other Interesting Books—Spirituality

God Within: *Our Spiritual Future—As Told by Today's New Adults*

Edited by *Jon M. Sweeney, Editor-in-Chief, SkyLight Paths*

Our faith, in our words.

The future of spirituality in America lies in the vision of the women and men who are the children of the "baby boomer" generation—born into the post-New-Age world of the 1970s and 80s. This book gives voice to their spiritual energy, and allows readers of all ages to share in their passionate quests for faith and belief. Sometimes irreverent—but alway~ ~·~le~ *—this thought-provoking collection of writings, poetry, and art sh   · voic~   ~g the future of religion, faith, and belief as   ·^ow i   3361-15-2 **$14.95**

Releasing t~   ~al   *Your Life*

by *Dan Wakef.*

From the author of *How Do We Know When It's God?*— a practical guide to accessing creative power in every area of your life.

In this passionate, personal guide, award-winning author Dan Wakefield explodes the myths associated with the creative process and shows how everyone can uncover and develop their natural ability to create. Drawing on religion, psychology, and the arts, he teaches us that the key to creation of any kind is clarity—of body, mind, and spirit—and he provides practical exercises that each of us can do to access that centered quality that allows creativity to shine. 7 x 10, 208 pp, Quality PB, ISBN 1-893361-36-5 **$16.95**

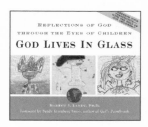

God Lives in Glass: *Reflections of God through the Eyes of Children*

by *Robert J. Landy, Ph.D.*;

Foreword by *Sandy Eisenberg Sasso*, author of *God's Paintbrush*

Children from around the world show us God in ways we may have forgotten.

How do kids imagine God? In many and diverse ways full of wonder and rebuke, in ways that grownups may have forgotten. In ways that you will be delighted to remember. This full-color book of insights celebrates the unique spirituality of children, allowing adults to take an eye-opening look at our own faith, religion, and spirituality—and to rediscover a fresh, enlightening perspective. 7 x 6, 64 pp, HC, Full-color illus. ISBN 1-893361-30-6 **$12.95**

Or phone, fax, mail or e-mail to: SKYLIGHT PATHS Publishing

Sunset Farm Offices, Route 4 • P.O. Box 237 • Woodstock, Vermont 05091

Tel: (802) 457-4000 • Fax: (802) 457-4004 • www.skylightpaths.com

Credit card orders: (800) 962-4544 (9AM–5PM ET Monday–Friday)

Generous discounts on quantity orders. Satisfaction guaranteed. Prices subject to change.